THROUGH THE SHADOWS WITH O.HENRY

WILLIAM SIDNEY PORTER

"O. HENRY," FROM A CRAYON DRAWING BY HEITMAN

THROUGH
THE
SHADOWS
WITH
O.HENRY

AL JENNINGS

Skyhorse Publishing

First published 1921 by the H. K. Fly Company

First Skyhorse Publishing edition 2016

Skyhorse Publishing books may be purchased in bulk at special discounts for sales promotion, corporate gifts, fund-raising, or educational purposes. Special editions can also be created to specifications. For details, contact the Special Sales Department, Skyhorse Publishing, 307 West 36th Street, 11th Floor, New York, NY 10018 or info@skyhorsepublishing.com.

Skyhorse® and Skyhorse Publishing® are registered trademarks of Skyhorse Publishing, Inc.®, a Delaware corporation.

Visit our website at www.skyhorsepublishing.com.

10 9 8 7 6 5 4 3 2 1

Library of Congress Cataloging-in-Publication Data is available on file.

ISBN: 978-1-63450-422-5
Ebook ISBN: 978-1-5107-0144-1

Cover design by Rain Saukas

Printed in the United States of America

TO MY DEAR FRIEND FREMONT OLDER

EDITOR "SAN FRANCISCO CALL"

In giving this volume to the public I am indebted to you, without whose aid and encouragement the book would never have been written. To you again are due my thanks for furnishing the valued assistance of Elenore Meherin who greatly aided in the preparation of the manuscript.

Devotedly yours,

AL JENNINGS.

CONTENTS

CHAPTER I
PAGE

A mothers flight; birth in a snowdrift; the drunken father's blow; the runaway boy; the fight in the shambles; abandoned on the prairie 11

CHAPTER II

Failure as a bootblack; a friendly foreman; the only kid on the range; flogged at the wagon-tongue; slaying of the foreman; vengeance on the assassin 17

CHAPTER III

Chuck-buyer for the Lazy Z; last journey to Las Cruces; shooting up a saloon; in the calaboose; arrival of the father 22

CHAPTER IV

Release from jail; quiet years in Virginia; study of law; a new migration to the West; brawl in court; news of death in the night 26

CHAPTER V

Shot from behind; agonies of remorse; death scene in the saloon; a father's rebuke to his son; vengeance delayed 31

CHAPTER VI

In the outlaws' country; acquittal of the assassins; a brother's rage; false accusation; the father's denunciation; refuge in the outlaws' camp 38

CHAPTER VII

Planning a holdup; terrors of a novice; the train-robbery; a bloodless victory; division of the spoils; new threat of peril 45

CHAPTER VIII

PAGE

Hunting the enemy; the convention at El Reno; drama in the town-hall; flight of the conspirators; pursuit to Guthrie; failure of the quest; "the range or the pen"   54

CHAPTER IX

Frank turns outlaw; the stickup of the Santa Fé; the threat of dynamite; crudity of bloodshed; the lure of easy money 59

CHAPTER X

In the Panhandle; a starving hostess; theft and chivalry; $35,000 clear; dawning of romance; two plucky girls; the escape in the tramp 64

CHAPTER XI

The meeting with O. Henry in Honduras; the celebration of the Fourth; quelling a revolution; a new flight; the girl on the beach 71

CHAPTER XII

Voyaging at leisure; the grand ball in Mexico City; O. Henry's gallantry; the don's rage; O. Henry saved from the Spaniard's knife 80

CHAPTER XIII

In California; the bank-robbery; O. Henry's refusal; purchase of a ranch; coming of the marshals; flight and pursuit; the trap; capture at last 90

CHAPTER XIV

In the Ohio Penitentiary; horrors of prison life; in and out of Bankers' Row; a visit from O. Henry, fellow-convict; promise of help 100

CHAPTER XV

Despair; attempt at escape; in the hell-hole; torture in the prison; the diamond thief's revenge; the flogging; hard labor; a message of hope from O. Henry . . 109

CONTENTS

CHAPTER XVI

PAGE

The new "main finger," a tuba solo; failure at prayer; transfer to the post-office; literary ambition; O. Henry writes a story 116

CHAPTER XVII

O. Henry, bohemian; the Recluse Club in the prison; the vanishing kitchen; the tragedy of Big Joe; effect on O. Henry; personality of a genius 126

CHAPTER XVIII

tory of convict Dick Price; grief for his mother; her visit to the prison; the safe-opening; promise of pardon 136

CHAPTER XIX

Interest of O. Henry; Price the original of Jimmy Valentine; the pardon denied; death of the cracksman; the mother at the prison gate 150

CHAPTER XX

The Prison Demon; the beast exhibited; magic of kindness; reclamation; tragedy of Ira Maralatt; meeting of father and daughter 159

CHAPTER XXI

Methods of O. Henry; his promotion; the singing of Sally Castleton; O. Henry's indifference; the explanation 183

CHAPTER XXII

Defiance of Foley the Goat; honesty hounded; O. Henry's scorn; disruption of the Recluse Club 206

CHAPTER XXIII

O. Henry's rage against corruption; zeal yields to prudence; a draft of the grafter's wine 224

CHAPTER XXIV

Tainted meat; O. Henry's morbid curiosity; his interview with the Kid on the eve of execution; the Kid's story; the death scene; innocence of the Kid 232

CHAPTER XXV   PAGE

Last days of O. Henry in prison; intimate details; his departure 250

CHAPTER XXVI

O. Henry's silence; a letter at last; the proposed story; Mark Hanna visits the prison; pardon; double-crossed; freedom 256

CHAPTER XXVII

Practice of law; invitation from O. Henry; visit to Roosevelt; citizenship rights restored; with O. Henry in New York; the writer as guide 269

CHAPTER XXVIII

Episodes of city nights; feeding the hungry; Mame and Sue; suicide of Sadie 280

CHAPTER XXIX

Quest for material; Pilsner and the Halberdier; suggestion of a story; dining with editors; tales of train-robberies; a mood of despair 290

CHAPTER XXX

Supper with a "star"; frank criticism; O. Henry's prodigality; Sue's return 299

CHAPTER XXXI

After two years; a wedding invitation; another visit to New York; delayed hospitality; in O. Henry's home; blackmail 308

CHAPTER XXXII

New Year's Eve; the last talk; "a missionary after all" . 316

THROUGH THE SHADOWS
WITH O. HENRY

CHAPTER I.

A mother's flight; birth in a snowdrift; the drunken father's blow; the runaway boy; the fight in the shambles; abandoned on the prairie.

A wilderness of snow—wind tearing like a ruffian through the white silence—the bleak pines setting up a sudden roar—a woman and four children hurrying through the waste.

And abruptly the woman stumbling exhausted against a little fence corner, and the four children screaming in terror at the strange new calamity that had overtaken them.

The woman was my mother—the four children, the oldest eight, the youngest two, were my brothers. I was born in that fence corner in the snow in Tazwell County, Virginia, November 25, 1863. My brothers ran wildly through the Big Basin of Burke's Gardens, crying for help. My mother lay there in a fainting collapse from her five days' flight from the Tennessee plantation.

The Union soldiers were swooping down on our plantation. My father, John Jennings, was a colonel in the Confederate army. He sent a courier warning my mother to leave everything, to take the children and to cross the border into Virginia. The old home would be fired by the rebel soldiers to prevent occupation by Union troops.

A few of the old negroes left with her. They were but an hour on the road. They looked back. The plantation was in flames. At the sight the frightened darkies fled. My mother and the four youngsters went on. Sixty miles they tramped, half running, half walking, and always beset with alarms. Frank was so little he had to be carried. Sometimes they were knee deep in slush, sometimes they were slipping in the mud. The raw wind cut to the bone. It was perhaps as terrible and as bitter a journey as a woman ever took.

I was born in a snow heap and reared in a barn. They picked my mother up and carried her in a rickety old cart to the mountains. Jack and Zeb, the two oldest, had sent their panicky clamor through the waste. A woodsman answered.

The loft of an old log-cabin church in the Blue Ridge Mountains was our home in those hungry years of the Civil War. We had nothing but poverty. There was never enough to eat. We heard no word from my father. Suddenly in 1865 he returned and we moved to Mariontown, Ill.

I remember our home there. I remember our habitual starvation. We lived in an empty tobacco barn. There was hardly a stick of furniture in the place. Frank and I used to run wild about the bare rooms. I know that I was always longing for, and dreaming of, good things to eat.

Before the war my father was a physician. A little

sign on our barn tempted a few patients to try his skill and gradually he built up a meager practice. All at once, it seemed, his reputation grew and he became quite a figure in the town. He had never studied law, but he was elected district attorney.

It was as though a fairy charm had been cast over us. And then my mother died. It broke the spell.

There was something grim and fighting and stubborn about her. In all the misery of our pinched days I never heard her complain. She was perhaps too strong. When she died it was like the tearing up of a prop. The home went to pieces.

Frank and I were the youngest. A pair of stray dogs we were, grubbing about in alleys, bunking on the top floor of an old storehouse, earning our living by gathering coal off the sandbars of the Ohio river. We sold it for 10 cents a bushel. Sometimes we made as much as 15 cents in two days. Then we would stuff ourselves with pies and doughnuts. Usually our dinner was an uncertain and movable feast. Nobody troubled about us. Nobody told us what to do or what to avoid. We were our own law.

We were little savages fighting to survive. Nothing in our lives made us aware of any obligations to others. It was hardly an ideal environment wherein to raise law-respecting citizens.

My father tried to keep some sort of a home for us, but he was often away for weeks at a time. One night Frank met me at the river. His eyes stuck out like a cat's in the dark. He grabbed me by the coat and made me run along with him. He stopped suddenly and pointed to a great, black lump huddled against the door of Shrieber's store.

"That's paw," he said. "He's asleep out there."

Shame like a hot wave swept over me. I wanted to get him away. I was fond of him and I didn't want the people in the town to know. I ran up and caught him by the shoulder. "Paw, get up, get up," I whispered.

He sat up, his face stupid with sleep. Then he saw me and struck out a furious blow that sent me reeling to the curb. White hot with anger and hurt affection, I got up and ran like a little maniac to the river.

I threw myself on the sandbar and beat the ground in a fury of resentment. I was crushed and enraged. I wanted to get away, to strike out alone.

I knew the boats like a river rat. They were loading freight. I crawled in among the boxes of the old *Fleetwood* and I got to Cincinnati as forlorn and wretched as any runaway kid.

But I was a little cranky. I made up my mind to be a musician. I could play the trombone. The Volks theatre, a cheap beer garden, took me on. I worked like a slave for four days. Saturday night I went around to the manager and asked for my pay. I was starved. I had only eaten what I could pick up. For four days I had haunted the saloon lunch counters. I used to sneak in, grab a sandwich, duck, grab another and get kicked out.

"You mangy little ragamuffin," the manager swore, with more oaths than I had ever heard before. "Get out of here!"

He knocked me against the wall. I had an old bull-dog pistol. I fired at him and ran.

The shot went wild. I saw that, but I saw, too,

that I had to run. I didn't stop until I had climbed onto a blind baggage car bound for St. Louis. Then I crept into a hog car, pulled the hay over me and slept until I was dumped off at the stockyards in Kansas City.

It was the first time I was on the dodge. It is an ugly thing for a boy of 11 to attempt murder, but self-protection was the only law I knew. Society might shelter other youngsters. I had had to fight for almost every crust I had eaten. I was forced to take the law in my own hands or be beaten down by the gaunt poverty that warped my early life.

It was fight that won me a brief home at the stockyards. I had a scrap with the kid terror of the shambles. We fought to a finish. Grown men stood about and shouted with laughter. Blood streamed from my nose and mouth. The fight was a draw.

The terror's father came over and shook my hand. I went home with them and stayed for a month. The kid and I would have died for each other in a week. We cleaned out every other youngster in the yard. The kid's mother, slovenly and intemperate as she was, had the sunny kindness of people that have hungered and suffered. She was like a mother to me.

On an old schooner wagon we started across the plains together. Near the little town of La Junta, came the catastrophe that wrecked my existence.

Al Brown got hold of some whiskey. We stopped for the night in the midst of the prairie. The beans were boiling in the open. He walked up to the fire, looked into the saucepan—"Beans, again," he snarled, and kicked the dinner to the ground. Without a word his wife took up the frying pan and beat him over the head. He went out—cold.

The kid and I had to run out to the edge of the prairie. We always did when they started to scrap.

She came out, hooked up the team and began dumping in her things and the kid's.

"Johnny, get your duds; we're going to leave," she said.

I never felt so isolated in my life. The kid didn't want to leave me. I started to cry. It was getting terribly dark. The woman came back. "Honey, I can't take you," she said.

I was afraid of the dark, afraid of the silence. I caught hold of her. She pushed me away, climbed up on the wagon and drove off, leaving me alone on the prairie with the man she thought she had murdered.

CHAPTER II.

Failure as a bootblack; a friendly foreman; the only kid on the range; flogged at the wagon-tongue; slaying of the foreman; vengeance on the assassin.

I sat there until the night, pulsing and heavy, seemed to fold in on me like a blanket. Then I rolled over on my face and groped along to the embers where Al Brown lay. I wanted company. I crouched down at his side and lay there. I was almost asleep when a queer thumping sent a shivering terror through me. I lay still and listened. It was Al Brown's heart beating against my ear.

The bells and whistles of all New York thundering to the New Year sent me crazy with delight the first time I heard them—the prison gate clanging to on me made me insolent with joy—but never was there a sound so good to hear as the pumping of Al Brown's heart.

I grabbed his hat and ran to the big buffalo wallow. Again and again I dashed the hatful of water in his face. Finally he lolled over to one side and struggled to his knees. "Which way'd she go?" He asked quietly enough, but I was suspicious. I pointed in the opposite direction. Al rubbed the blood from the side of his face. "Let her go," he said amiably, and went stumbling off toward the creek. I followed him. He turned about. "Go 'long, sonny," he said.

I waited till he took a few paces and then I sneaked

after him.   If Al Brown or his wife had stuck by me
then I don't believe I'd be Al Jennings, the outlaw,
today.   It made him angry to have me trailing him.
"See here, sonny, you go 'long—hustle for yourself!"

It was a mile across the curly mesquite flats to the
town of La Junta.   My heels were my only horses
then, but the bullets of a sheriff's posse never set me
sprinting the way that prairie darkness did.   I reached
the town just in time to catch special apartments
where the hay was clean and soft on a west-going
train.   It trundled into Trinidad, Colo., at 3 a. m.,
and I hung around the depot until morning casting
about for a business opening.

My opportunity came with a Mexican kid of my
own age.   He carried a bootblack kit.   I had a quarter.
We swapped and I set out with my brushes ready to
clean all the boots in the State.   But the Mex swin-
dled me.   The people in Trinidad never blacked their
shoes.   I shouted "Shine, shine" until my throat ached
and my stomach hooted with neglect.   I felt like a
menial.

At last I collared a patron.   A giant in a white
hat with a string hanging down in front and another
in back, a gray shirt, and sloppy, check trousers that
seemed to stick by a miracle to his hips, slouched my
way.

It was Jim Stanton, foreman of the 101 Ranch.
He had the longest nose, the hardest face and the
warmest heart of any man I ever knew.   Three years
later, when I was 14, Stanton was murdered.   I'd like
to have died that day.

My prospective patron wore boots with the long,

narrow heels, sloping toward the instep, that the cow-boys of that time wore. I wanted a closer squint at them.

I stood in his way and asked insultingly, "Shine?"

"Lo, Sandy, never had no paste on them yet; try it."

He didn't like my methods. The black stuck in mealy spots.

"Reckon you didn't daub it right, bub," he said.

"Go to hell, damn you," I told him.

"Pow'ful bad temper, sonny," he drawled. "How'd you like to be a cowboy?"

It was kid heaven opened to me. That night I took my first long ride. Jim Stanton fitted me out from head to foot. I had never sat a horse, but we went 60 miles without a stop. There wasn't a kid on the range. They gave me a man's work and a man's responsibilities. They made me the wrangler, and when I took to running the fifty horses over the hills they used cowboy discipline to teach me that horses should be walked in. They strung me out across the wagon tongue and beat me into insensibility.

After that beating I was an outcast. Nobody so much as noticed me. I longed for the Prairie Kid. I would have run away, but there was no place to go. The resentment that always riled me when the law went against me was burning my heart out. I hated them all.

I was sitting down by the corrals one day when Stanton came along. "Lo, Sandy, here's a new bridle with tassels on it. Get your horse." It was the first thing any one had said to me in three days and I just busted out crying.

I was Jim Stanton's man Friday after that. He came to trust me like the toughest man on the range. He treated me like a pal. Stanton taught me cowboy law and, except for the running of the horses in my early days, I never violated it. I was square as any fellow and was reckoned a valuable hand, though I was ten years younger than most of them.

Then came the tragedy that made me a "wild one." Some steers from the O-X ranch got mixed with ours. There was a dispute over the brands. Jim won his point, and the O-X peelers left without any particular ill-feeling.

Jim went down to the branding pen to look over the steers. I was standing about two hundred feet away when I heard a shot fired, and an instant later caught sight of Pedro, one of the O-X men, galloping off at a mad speed.

Villainy had been done. I knew it. I ran down to the pens. Jim was crouched over on his knees with a bullet hole in his back.

It was as though everything went dead within me. It was the first real grief I had ever known. I sat there holding Jim's hand when I should have been out after Pedro. I sat there mopping his blood off with a bandana when I should have been yelling for help. Jim was the only friend I had ever had—he was all but God to me.

To shoot a man from behind is crime in the cowboy code. The man who does it is a coward and a murderer. He is pursued and his punishment is death.

Pedro vanished from the face of the earth for a few months. We gave up the chase for him. One day Chicken, a kid of eighteen, came back from the hills. He had been watching our cattle to keep the steers from following a trail herd going north.

"Get your horse," he said. "I know where Pedro is —Presidio county on the Rio Grande."

We left that night with four horses and fifty dollars from Jim's successor. We rode six hundred miles and we got to Uncle Jimmy Ellison's on the Rio Grande just as the peelers were coming back from gathering horses for the spring work. They were running them into the corrals. I rode up and stood at the fence. Pedro came galloping up and into the corrals from the opposite side. He didn't see me. Like a flash I spurred in between the horses. They went wild and broke from the corral. Pedro turned, recognized me, and shouted to the men. I fired and caught him clean between the eyes.

CHAPTER III.

Chuck-buyer for the Lazy Z; last journey to Las Cruces; shooting up a saloon; in the calaboose; arrival of the father.

In the code of the cowboy, it was right that Pedro should die. I felt that I had done a magnificent thing to kill him. Kidlike I had a notion that Jim Stanton had watched and approved.

But we did not go back to 101. We hid in chaparral patches in the day, traveling nights until we reached the Lazy Z range near the Rio Verde. They made me chuck-buyer here. We had to go thirty-five miles across the desert to the town of Las Cruces for our provisions. It was about three months after the murder of Jim Stanton that I took my last ride through the gulches. In a mean and shameful predicament my father found me.

Old Spit-Nosed Ben, the superannuated relic of the Lazy Z, was with me on that last ride. He was a sort of errand boy on the ranch. We had loaded up the ancient double-decker freight wagon with about 1,600 pounds of chuck. Ben was hitching up the ponies. We were just ready to leave.

And then it occurred to me that I would get a drink. I was the youngest peeler on the Lazy Z. Chuck-buying was a man-size job, and I had a sense of great importance in it. A fellow in the grocery had gibed at me. "Eh, little gringo diablo, little wart, where did they pick you off?"

I wanted to prove myself. At the 101 the men had held me down. Jim had shoved me away from whiskey. I felt it was time to assert myself.

The saloon was a dingy, one-roomed Spanish adobe with an atmosphere of stale frijoles and green flies. There were a few Mexicans gambling rather idly and a couple of cowpunchers playing pool. I sauntered up to the bar and took a drink, ordered another and then a third. It was the first time in my life I had ever had more than one at a throw. It fired me in an instant. Just to let them know I was there I shot three bottles off the back bar. The old looking-glass came down with a crash, and I went plumb wild and started to pump the place full of lead. The Mexicans got scared and made for the back door. One of the cowpunchers caught his billiard cue across the door and the whole crowd were banked up there. I was reeling by this time and went to busting a few 45's at their feet.

Two shots were fired, just grazing the skin of my neck. I turned. The room was hung with the gray smoke cloud, and the whiskey had me reeling, but through the haze I saw the bartender aiming straight for my head. Two more shots went wild. I fired pointblank at the fellow's face. He went down.

It sobered me. I made for the door. A crowd of greasers clamored about me. My six-shooter was empty. As I got to the street some one smashed me across the head with a forty-five. I woke up in the calaboose.

I didn't know why I was there. I remembered nothing but the terrible crashing in my head. Then they told me that I had killed a man and asked me if I had any friends. Chicken was the only fellow on the range of whom I would ask a favor. He was a blind adder fighter and came in to finish up the town for me. I felt sure that he would get me out somehow.

The calaboose was a wooden pen about 8 x 10 feet. For six weeks I was kept there with Mexican Pete for my guard. Pete would sit in the sun outside the grating and describe my execution. He went into all its details. Every morning he strung me up in a different way. But he was a good sort. After the first week we were friends. Pete had all the Mexican treachery to the stranger and all their doglike fidelity to a friend.

They would have hanged me with as little compunction as they would have drowned an excess kitten, but they felt no hatred for me as a murderer. Life was reckoned cheap in the cow country.

One morning Pete stuck his head between the bars of the calaboose. His long yellow teeth gleamed. "Your padre, he come," he said.

It was as if lightning went through me. I thought that Pete was poking more fun at me. He repeated, "Your padre, big fellow, he come."

I would rather have been taken out to the tree and hanged. I did not want to see my father. I had that picture of him lying at Shrieber's store burned into my mind. But I had also the memory of a hundred gentle things he had done, balancing the roughness of that last impression. I did not want him to see me

in the pen with a Mexican standing guard over me.
For the first time I felt sorry for the whole affair.

It was Chicken who had sent for him. Once in a fit
of depression I had confided in him. We were out
on night herd together. The thick breath of the hot
evening weighed about us. The cattle had been restless, cracking their horns together, crowding and
scuffling. We had bedded them down at last on the
level prairie and there was that tremendous silence of
the night which rests like the hush of death over the
plains.

A storm was coming. We feared a stampede.
Chicken and I sat on our horses, riding slowly around
the cattle, singing to quiet them. We began to hear
the rolling boom of thunder. Lightning struck
through the darkness, darting its uncanny flash about
the horns of the steers.

I felt lonesome and homesick and full of premoni-
tions. Often since the death of Jim Stanton I had
thought of going back. I was tired of the isolation, of
the ranges. I wondered about my father and my
brothers. I wanted them to know if I died. This
night I told Chicken to write to my father's people in
Charleston, Va., if I should be killed.

Pete stood there grinning at me. Never in my life
have I felt so hot with shame and humiliation. I
wanted to escape. I came out from my corner to beg
Pete to free me. My father, straight, kind, smiling,
stood looking at me, his hand stretched through the
bars of the calaboose.

CHAPTER IV.

Release from jail; quiet years in Virginia; study of law; a new migration to the West; brawl in court; news of death in the night.

There was such a queer, gentle look in my father's face, as though he were the culprit and not I. It jabbed me to the quick. He never said a word of censure to me—not then nor in all the years that followed.

But he went quietly to work to win my release. Three days later I left Las Cruces with him. I was not even brought to trial. My father had taken a new start, studied law, won success, gathered the family about him and settled in Charleston, Virginia. The boys he sent to the Virginia Military academy. Frank and I finished the study of law four years later, when I was just past 18.

There must have been something unstable and reckless in our natures, for our lives never ran along the level. We seemed to court adversity. Our fortunes went like a wave through a continual succession of swells and hollows.

We struck the hollows when I finished college. The family packed its baggage and moved to Coldwater, Kansas.

The Middle West was wild, new country then. We moved from Kansas, took up land in Colorado, built the town of Boston, sold town lots, cleared $75,000 and lost every cent of it in the county-seat fight.

Crumb-clean we went into Oklahoma in 1889. The settlers were all bankrupt. The government even issued food to them. Frank and I were both athletes. We supported the family with the money we earned at foot racing.

Just about this time one of the periodic swells in our fortunes swept my father into Woodward county, where he was appointed judge by Governor Renfro. John and Ed opened law offices in the same town. I was elected county attorney of El Reno. Frank was deputy clerk in Denver.

It was the crest of our prosperity. Judge Jennings was the man of weight in the community. He was re-elected almost unanimously. John and Ed were the attorneys in every big case that came up in the courts. My father had built a beautiful home and had a comfortable bank account. We were going forward with a swift, sure current when the Garst affair, like the uncharted rock, blocked our course.

Many events in my life—the pistol shot in the Cincinnati theatre, the desertion in the prairies, the lawlessness of the ranges—seemed to have been shaping the channel for the rapids that were to hurl Frank and me into the maelstrom of robbery and murder. The Garst case precipitated the downfall.

Jack Love had been appointed sheriff at the same time my father was named judge. He was a gambler and a disreputable character. While in office he had a little habit of arresting the citizens and charging them an exit fee in order to get out of jail. He developed also a great penchant for land-grabbing, appropriating 50,000 acres of the government's property.

Frank Garst rented this land for the pasturage of 1,700 cattle. He agreed to pay Love $3,000. When the bill was presented it was greatly in excess of this sum. Garst refused to pay. Love brought suit. Temple Houston defended the interests of Love; my brother Ed was attorney for Garst.

Love came to Ed and offered him $1,000 in cash to dump Garst. Ed refused and won the case for his client. He won it on the ground that Love had no right to the land in the first place and was himself a trespasser.

Love was out his $3,000. He was a bad loser. Ed's fate was really sealed when he won that case. Love waited his chance.

It came a few weeks later. I went to Woodward to visit my father. Ed was defending a group of boys on a burglary charge. Temple Houston, Love's attorney, was prosecuting. Ed asked me to assist him. The case was going against Houston. The atmosphere was charged with bitterness. In the midst of my plea, Houston got to his feet, slammed his fist on the table and shouted, "Your honor, the gentleman is grossly ignorant of the law."

"You're a damn' liar," I answered, without any particular heat, but as one asserting an evident fact.

It was like a blow in the face to Houston. He lost all control of himself. "Take that back, you damn' little —— —— ——!" He hurled the unpardonable epithet, and sprang at me.

His face was bursting with rage. His hand was on his forty-five and I had mine leveled at him. Lightning anger was striking in all directions. Men rushed to the one side and the other. Somebody dashed the six-shooter from my hand. At the same moment I saw Houston surrounded and disarmed.

The court proceedings ended for the day. But feeling ran high—the white-hot fury of the Southern cow people. Nothing but blood cools it. We knew that the settlement must be made.

For once in my life I was not eager to square the account with killings. We went to Ed's office, my father and my two brothers. My father's harried face was like a reproach to our hot tempers. He was a broken man. He seemed to see the tragic failure of his life of robust endeavor.

"What are you going to do?" he asked, almost in an appeal.

"Nothing, until tomorrow," I told him, for I had made my plans. I intended to meet Houston, apologize for my insults, demand the same from him and let it go at that. If Houston refused it would be time enough to meet the issue.

My decision was not to be. The town was divided into two factions. Ours outnumbered Houston's two to one. They made up in their rankling animosity what they lacked in numbers. It was as if two tigers stood ready to spring and each but waited to get the other in a corner.

Ed and John agreed to stay in town to watch the office. I went home with my father.

Never had the magnetism of his kind, turbulent

nature seemed so forcible as in the weakness of his fear for us. He was in a reminiscent mood. For the first time he spoke of that day when he had struck me down at Shrieber's store. The tears crowded into his eyes. I knew that many a torturing moment had paid for that irresponsible blow.

At 10 o'clock we went to bed. It was a hot summer night. We left our doors open. I was just dropping into a slumber when I heard the stumble of frantic footsteps on the steps below. The door was pushed to and a broken voice called out:

"Judge, get up, get up, judge, quick; they have killed both your boys!"

CHAPTER V.

Shot from behind; agonies of remorse; death scene in the saloon; a
father's rebuke to his son; vengeance delayed.

"Killed both your boys!"

The broken cry seemed running up the stairs like
a distraught presence; pounding along the walls;
shaking through the doors. Its quiver beat through
the clamorous silence.

Thought stopped. My blood seemed to be running
into molten steel that was wrapping me in quick, hot
suffocation. I felt as though I were melting into a
lump of motionless terror.

My father's voice sprang through the hush—a
howl, tortured and agonized, that trailed into a whistling moan. It shot through me like a cold blade.
Livid, gray, helpless, his hands dropped to his sides,
his eyes like burnt holes in a white cloth, he slumped
against the door.

Half dressed, I ran past him, down the street
toward the saloon. Something black and hunched fell
against me. I put out my hand to strike it off.

"Only me—got Ed—cleaned out—hurry."

It was John. His face was a monstrous red stain.
His coat was drenched with blood. His left arm—
shattered from the shoulder.

"Hurry!" he gasped. "Go. I'm O. K. Only got

me in the shoulder. Ed's done up. Oh, for God's
sake, go and be quick about it."

Ed was dead. John was dying. My father broken-
hearted.

And all thanks to me! Never was anybody so
whipped with remorse, so crushed. Pretty work my
crude violence had done at last! My unbridled temper
was the real murderer. If I had not come on this
visit! If I had only stayed on the range! If they
had only hanged me in Las Cruces! Like a pack of
hounds the bitter thoughts kept baying at me as I
went that quarter of a mile to the saloon.

When I lunged through that door the crowd
snapped apart like a taut string. Some scooted under
the gambling table—others made for the door. The
place was cleared.

And there on the floor, lying in a huge blot of warm
blood, his face downward, was my brother Ed. He
had been shot through the head, just at the base of the
brain.

All that was good and human and soft in me rushed
into my throat, cried itself out and died that hour that
I sat there with Ed's head in my lap and his blood
soaked into my hands and my clothes. Death was
stealing into my soul with a blight more fatal than
the wrecking of my brother's body.

No one spoke—no one put out a hand to me, until
presently the doctor leaned forward. "Al, let me
do something; get up now."

At the words the saloon was suddenly a-hum with
voices. Men crowded about me. Sentences seemed to
rush from them like pebbles down a cliff.

"He was right there—playing pitch," some one began. Another and another interrupted.

"They struck from behind—"

"They sneaked in—"

"They soaked him when he was down—"

"They pumped John—"

"They beat it like coyotes—"

And then they put it all together and told it again and again from the beginning.

The saloon was the two-room wooden shack with bar and gambling house combined, the common type in the Middle West a quarter of a century ago. Ed was playing pitch at one of the little side tables in the gambling-room. At one end of this room the town band was giving a concert. A score of crap shooters were busy on either side.

Temple Houston and Jack Love came in by the back door, passed in front of the band and separated, Houston going toward Ed, Love sneaking, unseen, behind his table. Both men were drunk.

"Are you going to apologize?" Houston blubbered. Ed turned and faced him. His back was to Love.

"When you're sober come back. Apologies will be settled then."

"That's all I wanted to know," Houston answered, shuffling off. At the same instant Love jammed his forty-five against Ed's head and fired. As he dropped, Houston rushed up and pumped two bullets into my brother's skull.

When the shooting broke the gamblers barricaded themselves behind the tables. Men in the bar-room scurried into the street. John was standing outside.

He rushed in as Ed fell. Half way across the outer room Houston and Love caught him with a full volley. Before anyone recovered from the sudden panic the murderers were gone.

They brought Ed home. John lay dying. My father sat up and watched. I could not go near the house. I went out to the barn and waited. I felt like another Cain.

There was no indecision in my mind. I knew that my lawless temper had precipitated the killing. But Love had been laying for Ed. He had ribbed Houston to the shooting. They had murdered deliberately, cowardly—they had shot from behind.

Before the night was over the news went like a flame through the country. Woodward held its breath and waited for the answering shot.

Houston and Love would come back. They expected me to get them.

The remorse of the night before had reared like a coiled snake into a poisonous vengeance. There would be no quitting now.

The mean, sordid gray of early morning had just streaked the night sky. My father came out to the barn. He looked tall and grim, but blanched as a leper.

"Come in with me." His voice seemed pressed and flattened with misery. "Come in here." He led the way to the room where John lay in a moaning delirium.

"There's one," he pointed.

And then he moved silently into the other room where Ed had been placed on the board table.

My father's cavernous eyes glowed into mine in a blazing scrutiny.

"There's two," he said.

"Now what are you going to do? Are you going to finish us?"

It was like a whiplash cutting a welt across my face. I felt like a beaten, cowering dog.

Neither of us spoke. It was hard even to breathe. I could see that my father's hand trembled. I did not want to look into his accusing face.

What did he mean? Did he expect me to do nothing, while all of Woodward waited for the blow?

He knew the spirit of these prairie towns. Men settled their own accounts in swift and deadly fashion. Ex-fugitives and old range men made up the population. They paid little tribute to the law.

The marshals who administered it were the meanest men in the country. They were mostly former horse-thieves, rustlers or renegade gamblers.

The outlaws did their financeering with a six-shooter; the marshals used a whiskey bottle.

I have known deputy U. S. marshals, dozens of times, deliberately sneak the bottle into the schooner wagons going across the plains; double back on the occupants, search the wagons, find the bottle, tie their victims to the trees, hold them until the scoundrelly trick gave them about 10 prisoners. Then they would drive them all into Fort Smith, produce their fraudulent evidence, collect mileage and cold-bloodedly have those innocent men sent up for four or five years on the charge of introducing liquor into the Indian Territory. Ohio penitentiary, when I landed there, was choked with men serving time on such trumped-up cases.

The marshals grabbed off about $2,000 on the deal. The cowpunchers who sometimes became outlaws were clean men by comparison. They took little stock in the justice of sneak thieves.

These things I knew. It was not murder to strike down the men who had shot from the back. In the Middle West, it was honor.

It was not honor that I wanted, but vengeance. Ed and I had been 12 years together. He had taken the place of Stanton, of Chicken. He was more than either to me. Big natured, clear brained, the gentlest fellow that ever lived—and there he was with the back of his poor head blown off with the murderous bullets.

"Listen to me!" My father's voice seemed rumbling through a wall of pain. It jerked me back. "Listen to me. There's been killing enough. There's been sorrow enough.

"Your brother has paid the penalty of vengeance. John, too, may pay. Where will it end? When Woodward runs with blood?"

He went on as though he were possessed.

"You shall not do it. I am the judge here. I was appointed when the county was formed. I was named to maintain the law. If my own sons will not stand by me what can I expect from others?"

All of a sudden he stopped. His colorless face seemed crumpled with misery. "Al, you won't do anything till Frank comes, will you?"

Frank came on from Denver. My father had his way.

"Let them go to trial," Frank said. "He wants it. I'll do no killing."

Frank was always like that, impulsive, soft-hearted, generous—undecided until he got into action, then he tore ahead deadly and relentless as a very hell on wheels. As for myself, I felt a blazing hatred against them all in my heart. I made one promise. I would wait until the trial was over. If the law failed, I would strike.

But we could not stay in Woodward. Not even the old gentleman could stand that. He took John down to Tecumseh and almost immediately was named a judge there. Frank and I went to the sheriff, Tob Olden, and told him we would wait. He was disappointed.

"May want to hit the bull's eye later, boys. When you reckon to bust them off, Tob Olden's house is yours."

CHAPTER VI

In the outlaws' country; acquittal of the assassins; a brother's rage; false accusation; the father's denunciation; refuge in the outlaw's camp.

Nearly every range on the prairies sheltered and winked at outlaw gangs. From peeler to highwayman was a short step.

Frank and I went down to the Spike S to hang up till after the trial.

John Harliss owned the ranch. The Snake Creek and the Arkansas river ran through his 100,000 acres. It was an ideal haunt for fugitives. Harliss was hospitable. The Conchorda Mountains, like tremendous black towers, formed a massive wall on one side. The cliff came down to the creek. On the near side of the water the land rolled out in a magnificent sweep of low hills and valleys.

Once across the Snake Creek to the mountain side, and capture was almost impossible. Dogwood, pecan trees, briar and cottonwood matted together and spread like a jungle growth up the mountain and there wasn't a marshal in the State would set a horse toward it.

It was across the Snake Creek and up the Conchorda that I made my last race against the law, years later.

I went cow-punching there; Frank went over to Pryor's Creek, 20 miles distant.

The branding pen was just at the edge of the timber on the near side of the creek. Harliss was not over-particular as to the ownership of the calves branded. His pen was well concealed.

One morning we were branding the cattle. Five men rode up, nodded to Harliss and began stripping off the meat from the carcass hanging in the trees. One of them came over to me.

"Reckon you don't remember me? Reckon you uster work on the Lazy Z for my father?"

He knew of the shooting in Las Cruces. He knew of my brother's murder. He knew I had a fast gun and a close mouth. He told me of a robbery that had been pulled off on the Sante Fe.

"Ain't much in range work," he ended. "Reckon you'll join us yet."

He was a shrewd prophet. Not more than a month later John Harliss was sitting on the porch of the ranch house. I was standing in the door. A nester rode up. We knew that something had happened.

The nester comes only to bring news. If there's one fellow in the world that loves gossip it's these puffy little farmers that nestle in the flats. It makes them big with importance.

John Harliss was a blond giant. He towered over the blustering nester.

"Ain't heard the news, hev ye?" Then he caught sight of me and added furtively. "They cleared the fellows that killed Jennings' brother."

Houston and Love free!

The thing I had been dreading and expecting for six months came now with a shock that sent a cold fury of resolution through me. I knew that I would have to do deliberately what I should have done in passion.

It was not blood-lust, but raging vindictiveness that spurred me on the 75-mile ride to my father's house.

The hoofbeats stopping at his door aroused him. When he saw me, he stood as one petrified.

"Lo, your honor!" I put out my hand. He did not take it.

"What have you been doing?" Never had I seen his eye so cold, so hostile. "What does this mean?" He reached into his pocket, took out a folded handbill and offered it for me to read.

"Reward for the apprehension of Al Jennings," it said, "wanted for the robbery of the Santa Fe Express."

I saw it in a moment. That was the work of Houston and Love. They would get me out of the way. They would save their cringing hides by another cowardly attack.

"I had nothing to do with it. I'm damn' sorry I didn't——" I hurled the words at my father. Anger caught me by the throat and was choking me. "Damned if I had anything to do with it. By hell, they'll pay for it."

"If you had nothing to do with it, give up and clear yourself. That's the way to make them pay."

One of those sudden shifts from command to appeal softened my father's face. "Do you want to bring disgrace on the name?" he asked.

"The name be damned and the law and everything connected with it. I hate it."

"If you don't come in and clear yourself, I'm finished with you."

"I can't clear myself," I told him. "The Harliss
range harbors outlaws. I can't bring them in to prove
an alibi for me. Harliss wasn't there at the time. If
I did give up, I couldn't establish my innocence."

"Then you're guilty?"

Not in all the lawlessness of my early life, nor in
all the frenzy of sorrow and revenge after the murder, had such a full tide of storming violence beaten
down the discretion of my nature. If he distrusted
me what had I to expect from enemies?

I went out from my father's house, lashed with a
desperate, unappeasable fury. I wanted something
to happen that once and for all would put me beyond
the pale.

I slept out on the range and the next morning rode
toward Arbeka. I had eaten nothing the day before.
On the public road through the timber on the old
trail west from Fort Smith was a little country store.
I could have carried off nearly all its contents in my
slicker.

Five men were lounging on the bench near the horse
rack when I threw my bridle over the pole. Their
horses were tied. I couldn't tell whether they were
marshals or horse-thieves from the look of them.
Whatever difference there is favors the horse-thief.

I bought some cheese and crackers. When I came
out my horse was gone.

"Where's my horse?" The fellow felt the hot blast
of anger in the challenge.

"Ran away," he answered.

"Ran?" I snapped at him. "Some of you fellows turned him loose."

In the glade about 200 yards distant, I saw my horse nibbling grass. I ran down, mounted and was just galloping off when a shot whizzed past, then a clash, a volley, and the next moment the horse lunged sideward and thumped to the ground, pinning my leg under him.

They were possemen out to get me on the holdup. They were five to one and they didn't even try to take me on the porch. They fired without calling for a surrender. It was better to get a suspected train-robber dead than alive. The question of guilt and the surety of reward were then settled beyond dispute.

I pulled myself free, started firing like a madman, and saw two of them drop. I hid behind a tree, reloaded and went for the porch, shooting as I went. Two of them ran into the timber.

As I got to the store the fifth tumbled over into the brush. I ran inside, took up an ax and smashed the place to pieces. The owner crawled out from behind an empty cider barrel. I didn't care what I did. The viciousness of their attack infuriated me. I busted one at him as he crawled out the back door.

The drawer in the counter was open. There was $27.50 in it. I took it. I needed no money, but the theft filled me with happiness. I had taken a definite step. I was a criminal now. My choice was made. I was one with the outlaws. For the first time since Ed's death, I felt at peace. I knew that I would have a gang with me now to the end.

The big iron-gray horse that had stood undisturbed

during the ruckus, I mounted and started back to the
Harliss ranch. My foot was slipping up and down
in my boot. I looked down.

The boot was filled with blood. One of the bullets
had struck through the muscles above my ankle. I
picked it out with my pen-knife and stuffed the hole
with a puff-ball weed.

When I got to the range I did not stop at the house
but made for the cover in the timber. As I came near
a pang of fear shot through me. It was long past
midnight, but they had a fire blazing. One of the men
raised himself stealthily and glanced toward me.

He nodded.

The sudden elation at the store was dissipated.
Should I go on? Could I rely on these men? I no
longer felt at ease with them. Should I tell them
what had happened? The silence of the fugitive is
inbred. The reserve of the savage in his armor. Innocent, I had trusted the outlaws; guilty, I doubted
their loyalty.

"Hello," Andy called.

"I'm coming over," I answered, guiding my horse
into the deep stream.

"Want some coffee?" Jake asked. I was limping
miserably. They asked no question.

"Looks like you got snagged," Bill offered.

"Got shot. They tried to kill me. Soaked my
horse full of lead. They beat it. I robbed the damned
store."

"Reckon you're with us."

Andy settled it.

They had a cozy camp hidden there in the lap of

the mountains. An old wagon sheet, stretched between two poles, roofed the kitchen. Bill was making biscuits in the flour sack, shuffling up just enough dough and not wetting the rest.

I was lying on the ground at the fire. A man on horseback in the level at the edge of the creek had reined in and sat staring at me.

Andy nodded to him. He came over. It was Bob, the fourth man of the gang.

"It's O. K.," he said. "She stops at the tank."

CHAPTER VII

Planning a holdup; terrors of a novice; the train-robbery; a bloodless victory; division of the spoils; new threat of peril.

"She rolls in at 11:25. We'll get the old man to dump her.

"And if it ain't there, we'll have to take up a collection from the passengers."

They sat under the wagon sheet, stowing in the biscuits and coolly doping out the "medicine."

I was getting soft in the backbone. I hadn't figured to jump right into a train-robbery. Here were four men deliberately planning to stick up an express car as leisurely as a batch of Wall-street brokers hatching out a legitimate steal. Little quivering arrows of nervousness went pricking through me. I felt that I had cast in my lot with Andy and his gang too hastily. The darkness fretted me. I began casting about for an alibi.

"Broke?" I asked. "I have some money. I've got $327. It's yours."

Andy flipped his fingers. Nobody else paid the slightest attention to the offer. Five men were better than four. I was committed. The M. K. T. was due to be robbed at 11:25 on the following night as she chugged across the bridge on the Verdigras river north of the Muskogee. The crossing was about 40 miles from the Spike S ranch.

Toward morning we turned in. I was the only one who didn't sleep. Andy told me afterward that green hands always feel the yellow streak the first time. When the light came sneaking through the clouds, I began to feel better. The oppression of the night is an uncanny thing to a man beset with fearful indecisions.

There wasn't another word said about the holdup. We lolled about and let the horses take their ease until the late afternoon. I was anxious to be on the road —to have the suspense over—to start the scrap and be done with it.

We mounted about 3 o'clock in the afternoon and made ahead at an amiable trot, stopping now and then to rest. We wanted to keep the horses cool for the return. It was coal dark when we rode into a clump of timber, tied one of the horses to a cottonwood tree and threw the other bridles over his saddle horn. It all helps in the getaway.

As soon as we climbed down through the brush, the terror of the night before, a thousand times intensified, jabbed through me. The branches of every tree rustled with alarms. I expected any moment to see marshals step from behind the trunks or angry citizens swoop down on us. The nearest house was five miles distant and the only living soul around, the old pump man. But the dry sticks crackled like a festive bonfire. I wanted to caution them to pick their way.

I felt as though the entire responsibility rested on my shoulders. It occurred to me the whole affair had been bungled. They had not planned it out enough.

"Suppose the old man won't stop the train?" the question popped out. Andy laughed in my ear.

"Then they'll have to get a new man at the pump house," he confided.

This put a crimp in me. I had shot men without any particular grudge, but to murder in cold blood as a matter of business—I'd have given anything on God's green earth to be off the job.

"Who's got a match?" Jake chirped as merrily as though he sat in his own dining-room.

"For God's sake, you're not going to strike a match here, are you?" Even the hoarse whisper seemed to boom through the silence. Jake struck the match, covering the light with his coat. He took out his watch. It was just 11:10. Fifteen minutes and the train would roll in.

The massive iron bridge all but crashed to pieces as I put a light foot on its beams. The tall girders heaved together. In a panic, I lost my footing and half slipped through the trestle. Andy scooped his hand down and grabbed me up as though I were a kitten.

Our plan was to stop the train on the middle of the bridge to prevent the passengers from getting out. We would stall these cars on the trestle; the express would halt at the tank. We could rifle it and make a getaway before any alarm could be sent.

Andy gave the orders.

"Bob, go bring the old man down and drag a red light along.

"Jake, you and Bill get on that side—Al and I will take the right. We need all the men tonight."

As Bob sauntered off, I wondered if I would ever see him again. He came back, chugging the old man in the back with his six-shooter and ribbing him as he came.

"Don't fall on this gun, Bub, or someone will do a slow walk tomorrow." The old fellow was chattering with fear.

"Be easy, lad; be easy, be easy," he kept repeating like a magpie. "I ain't a-going to kick a ruckus; be easy."

Suddenly there came a rumbling and a singing of the rails. Andy and I flopped to our sides. A light like a great eye flashed through the timber. The engine chugged viciously, heaved, whistled for the tank and stopped.

Stopped of its own accord for water before it even got to the bridge! I got ringy from head to foot and was rolling in the grass when a shot banged out and a man swinging a light jumped off the train. It was the conductor. He dashed right past me. I never thought to stop him. Andy ran past and fired. I came, too, then and began running and yelling up and down the tracks. Bill and Jake were firing and hollering on the other side of the train like an army of maniacs.

"Keep it up; that's it—" Andy yelled to me.

I did. Two or three passengers started to the steps. I fired in the air. They ducked. The fun was getting hot and furious. I was as happy as a drunkard.

And then the engine began to heave and the train pulled out. I was afraid of nothing. I wanted to run after it and kick it good-bye. I felt like bellowing. I wanted everyone to know I had stuck up a train and done it wonderfully.

The hush seemed to swallow us up. Out of the darkness I could feel Andy and Bob coming toward us. They didn't say a word. We started back quietly. I began to wonder what it was all about.

"Didn't get a bean?" I ventured. Andy caught my arm.

"Hell, yes, we went into the express," he said. "We got a little bundle."

I didn't even know they had gone into the express. I didn't know they had taken a cent. I was so caught up in a frenzy of excitement and suspense, I hadn't an inkling of Andy's maneuvers.

He had ordered the engineer out. Bob had cornered the express messenger. The two were as mild as lambs. They did more than they were told. The messenger opened up the safe and handed over the winnings.

I asked no more. I wanted to feel like an oldtimer. But I went across that bridge as though my feet were winged. I didn't fall through the trestle this time. The girders didn't cram about me and I never noticed whether the water was black or yellow. I was filled with a thrill of great achievement.

A few shots had been fired in the air, but not a man had been hurt, not a blow struck and here we were galloping back with a bundle of boodle in our slickers. The whole job had taken little more than half an hour. We struck into the timber of our encampment well before daylight.

The boys flopped down on the grass. Jake and I

stirred up a fire and put on a pot of coffee. I was obsessed with curiosity. I wanted to know what we had got—if it had been worth our while. Jake talked and talked. He didn't say one word about the stickup. He chewed on about old times on the Red Fork, about his kid days, about every fool thing but the holdup. I was bitten with eagerness.

Nobody else seemed worried about the profits. They gulped down coffee and stripped off meat as though eating were the one business of life. I began to fear that the reckoning would be postponed until the next day. Andy stretched himself, yawned and leisurely pointed to the horses.

"Bill, go over to my saddle-bag," he said, at last. "We might as well split this now."

I started up, knocking over the coffee pot. I had an idea it would take two men to carry the boodle. Andy grinned and rubbed his chin on his shoulder. No kid opening a Christmas package ever felt a happier shiver of excitement than I when that bundle was called for.

We were lying around the fire. Its flicker in the gray darkness caught the faces of the men in a ruddy glow. There were two packages. Both were small. Andy took one, opened it and emptied a lot of cheap jewelry into his hat.

Little blue and red stones flashed—gold necklaces glinted; ponderous watches ticked almost as loud as alarms. I lay there fascinated as though the jewels of an enchanted treasure chest were sparkling in the firelight.

Andy lumped them into five piles, opened the other

package and counted out $6,000 in currency. I felt a chill of disappointment; $600,000 would have been closer to my expectations.

To a copper, the pile was divided. Each man got $1,200 and a handful of trinkets. I jammed these spoils into my pocket with a rapture no attorney's fee had ever given me. I had earned as much in half an hour of gripping excitement as a year's labor as county attorney had given me!

Years later, when I was in the Ohio Penitentiary and O. Henry had been released and was struggling for success in New York, I wrote him the details of this holdup and added a lot of incidents from other jobs. I wanted to write a short story about it.

O. Henry was Bill Porter in those days. When he left the penitentiary he slammed the door on his past. He went to New York burning with the shame of his imprisonment and determined to hide his identity behind the name of O. Henry. Billy Raidler, a fellow convict, and I were about the only ones who knew him as an ex-con. The three of us were pals in the pen. Raidler was despondent—a typical jailbird pessimist. In every letter Porter wrote he urged me to stick by Billy, to remind him that two people in the world believed in him.

In answer to my letter he sent me detailed instructions. He told me just how to write the "Holdup." I did the best I could and sent the manuscript to him. He waved the O. Henry wand over it, turned it into a real story and sold it to *Everybody's*. It was one of his first successes. We went 50-50 on the profits.

By the time that story was written I had learned

that the drawbacks of the game outweigh a thousand to one the thrills. That first stickup was pulled off too successfully. It made me cocksure.

I had been forced into outlawry by the unwarranted attack at the Arbeka store. I knew the Southwest well enough to see that I would be railroaded to the penitentiary on the word of the marshals, as scores had been before. I went into the game unwillingly and was immediately captivated by its intensity—its apparent security. Revenge gave place to recklessness.

Not a rumor of the holdup reached the ranch. We lay around for days. Andy went off on his own hook. Bill slipped out a week later. Jake, Bob and I went up to the ranch house. A month had passed. We were not suspected. We decided to pull off another wad.

I wanted to get the Santa Fe. That was the charge in the handbill my father had shown me. I was condemned on that score already. I might as well have the boodle.

We were planning it one night at the ranch house. Harliss had gone to town. It was very late.

"What's that?" Jack started up.

Through the quiet, like heavy drumbeats pounding along the road, came the sound of a single galloping horse. We knew it must be a peeler. Possemen never travel alone.

At the porch he drew up. It was Frank.

I had not seen him since the news of the trial came. The old, bonny gladness was gone from his face.

"They've freed them! You heard it?"

Like a slap in the face, his haggard look struck me. He leaned forward, and lowered his voice.

"Hush," he whispered. "I've got the goods. Get to your horse, quick. The lousy cutthroats have put up a deal. They'll stop at nothing. They've got a posse after you."

CHAPTER VIII

Hunting the enemy; the convention at El Reno; drama in the town-hall;
flight of the conspirators; pursuit to Guthrie; failure of the
quest; "the range or the pen."

Relentless as the Corsican vendettas were these
early feuds in the Oklahoma and Indian Territory.
In the bad lands of the Southwest the roughest men
in the country had their dugouts. They scattered
all over the ranges. They killed. Other killers in
the jury freed them. The dead man was finished—
why bother the living about it? The living had taken
their chance. That was the Oklahoma logic of justice
in the early nineties. The law went with one party or
the other. It was a case of grab the John Doe warrants and go after your man.

Houston and Love had doped it up with the marshals. They were out to get us before we had a
chance to get them.

"We're going to El Reno," Frank said. "They
want blood. Let it be theirs. Change the brand.
They've had enough of ours."

I had not expected Frank to start things. He had
an easy-going way that was full of disdainful contempt
for the quick killers of the Houston and Love type.

"Here's the odds," he explained at last. "They're
going to hound us off the earth. The damn' cowards
have been on the dodge from us ever since they fin-

ished Ed. They've got all the guns in Woodward cocked against us.

"They've gone mad. They've plastered the country with handbills. They've got you down for the stickup of the Santa Fe. They've got a posse running up and down the country on the track of Al Jennings, the train-robber. They'll sock you off at sight!"

He dashed the words out—sharp, vicious. The money in my pocket suddenly weighed heavy as though it were the $600,000 I had dreamed of.

"They're a few days ahead of their guess—it was the M. K. T. I stuck." I wanted him to know. I didn't know how to tell it. I tried to make my voice indifferent and careless.

"Pretty neat, wasn't it?" His tone was as casual as mine. "They never left a footprint after them. Must have been old hands at the game."

"All but me," I answered. "Andy's gang are all vets."

"Damn' humorous you're feeling; damn' funny layout, ain't it?" He gave a whistle of impatience that acted like a spur to his horse. What my father had so readily accepted as true Frank would not even consider.

Even when I told him the whole affair he could scarcely credit it. "You really had nothing to do with it," he said. "You just went along. It was force of circumstances. Just a spectator, that's all. You had no right to take the money."

He did not know that less than a fortnight later he would himself jump into the lead of the biggest stickup job that had been pulled in the territory for years. His one thought was to get to El Reno for the opening of the Democratic convention, to get Houston and Love before they had a chance to railroad us to the penitentiary or to kill us.

"Once they get us, they'll finish it proper. They'll take a final swipe at the old man and John."

We got to El Reno in the afternoon; the train was to bring the delegates in at 10 o'clock that night. We kept under cover until it was time to go down to the station. There were small groups standing around. Everybody in the town knew me. I had been county attorney there for two years.

As we came along a dozen greeted us as friends. They knew why we came. They had seen the handbills. No one made any attempt to gather in the reward.

The train rolled in. Some one brushed past me.

"They've slipped," he said. "Bill Tillman saw you. Tipped them off."

The bourbons, old cowboys, ex-outlaws, nesters and a sprinkling of respectable citizens got off the train. Houston and Love were not among them. Two days later I met Tob Oden, sheriff of Woodward county.

"They've sneaked in," he said. "They're at the session now.

I didn't wait to get Frank.

The town-hall was crowded. An old friend of mine, Leslie Ross, was acting as chairman. I stood in the doorway waiting my chance to saunter in unobserved. A fellow in the middle of the room interrupted the speaker. Somebody else yelled for him to shut up; a man behind tried to jam him back in his chair—there was just enough of a ruckus.

I walked down the aisle, not missing a face. I was so intent I did not notice the breathless quiet that suddenly held the spectators. I glanced to the platform. Ross was standing with his hand upraised, his eyes riveted on me, his face ashen like a man on the verge of collapse. His look held the audience as a ghost might have.

"Gentlemen, a moment, keep your seats." He started walking down the steps and toward the aisle. "Just a moment," he repeated, rushing up to me. "I see a dear friend of mine."

"They're not here, Al," he whispered to me. "I swear to God, they haven't shown a face around. Don't start anything. Calm down."

He was more excited than I. He seemed to think I was ready to shoot up the place. Houston and Love were not there. They had skipped to Guthrie. Frank and I followed them.

We had come to the edge of the city. A man on horseback rode up to us. It was Ed Nicks, United States marshal.

"Don't go in, boys," he said. "They're laying for you. They've got warrants. They'll get you on that frameup. The trap is all set. They know you're coming. Half the men in Guthrie are armed against you. They'll harvest you the moment you set foot inside the town."

I had known Ed Nicks for 10 years. He was on the square.

We didn't get Houston and Love. They got us. They got us to the tune of a life term in prison and 10 years in addition. We'd be there yet if President McKinley had not commuted our sentence. They'd have brought us back on other charges if Theodore Roosevelt had not granted us a full pardon.

Nicks rode with us a mile.

"They've bought up the county, boys," he said. "You haven't a chance. Take your choice—the range or the pen."

CHAPTER IX

Fate had more than half a hand in the chance that turned Frank into a train-robber.

Ruffled and angry that our plan had failed, he turned on me when Nicks left. "I don't believe him," he said. "We should have gone on. We did not work it right. I'd like to see their posse.

He did not have long to wait. We stopped off for a bite with Nigger Amos. Amos was a giant with a face as black as pitch and a soul as white as snow. He had married the prettiest little mulatto in the country. Their home was a jaunty yellow cottage that sat in the midst of the cornfields. Amos and Collie were smiles from the heart out.

Whatever he had was ours. Collie was proud of her dishes and her cooking. Amos sat on the porch while she fried chicken and waited on us. We had come in just as the two were about to eat, and there was Amos, big, hard-working farmer, slinking into the background until after the white folk had their dinner.

"Let's call him in," I said to Frank. He dropped his fork in surprise, looking at me as though I were demented.

"Why not? Here's me, a highwayman—a train-robber; there's Amos, black skin, clean soul—why not? It's his grub anyway—

"Amos, come in and have dinner with us," I shouted to him. Poor Amos was more startled than Frank.

"What, sah? No, sah; no, sah; 'lowed I ain't forgot my manners."

Amos' manners probably saved our lives.

"Yo' boys done been up to mischief?" The whites of his eyes seemed ready to pop loose from the black when he looked into the room a second later. "What you done?" he panted. "Possemen a-comin'!"

Without waiting for an answer he ran to our horses and raced them into the cornfields.

"Yo' boys git down thar, too."

Not a moment too soon, for seven men galloped over the brow of the hill and drew rein at the porch. The innocence of Amos would have made an angel blush. He had seen no one. No, sah, no gemmen stopped at his door. Not one of them would dare to ride down to the cornfield in search of quarry. They cursed and browbeat him. Amos stood firm.

"What do you make of it?" Frank's impulsive, open face was blanched with anger. He was like a cornered beast, ready to strike at anything.

"What do you make of it?" he demanded again. "Well, I'll tell you. They've made the Santa Fe believe you robbed them. The Santa Fe is behind this."

It was probably a wild supposition. It seemed credible to us. Houston was attorney for the railroad. From the time we left the negro's cottage until we arrived at the Harliss ranch a few days later the posse was on our trail. It didn't worry me much. There was a tang of adventure in it that appealed. To Frank it was hell's torment. He didn't like being hunted. He seemed to feel there was all the shame of cowardice in the attempt to escape. It lashed him into a seething rage that made him want to turn and strike back at his pursuers.

They had been to the ranch house in our absence. They had left their mark in a few bullet holes in the walls.

"What are you going to do?" Frank asked. I was neither angry nor unhappy. Just then, outlawry as a business suited me.

"Finish up the deal Jake and I were planning when you came," I said.

"I'm with you."

And from that moment until the night of the hold-up he was like a man possessed. He had the resolution of an army behind him. Almost single-handed he pulled off the stickup of the Santa Fe. He had worked one vacation on the railroad. He knew all about engines, he said, because he had ridden the goat around the yards. He insisted on bringing up the train.

The Santa Fe stopped at Berwyn in the Chickasha. Frank and Bill were to get on the blind baggage as she drew out, climb over the coal tender and get the engineer and fireman. They were to bring the train about three-quarters of a mile into the timber where Jake, Little Dick and I were waiting. We would finish the transaction.

There was nothing spectacular about the job except the haul. It came off just as we planned it. A six-shooter is a commander that few men dare to question. When Frank jabbed it in the neck of the engineer he was master of the train. I stood on the track and waved my hand. Frank gave the order. The engineer stopped.

Little Dick and Jake ran up and down quieting the passengers with a big show of gun fire and much shattered glass. Few men are ever killed in a holdup. Veterans consider bloodshed bad form. Whenever I read of a conductor or messenger fatally shot I know that a new hand is in the game. It's easy to buffalo the crew. The passengers are a cinch to handle. They know the holdup has the drop on them. Nobody wants to take the chance of starting things. If they ever did break loose at the same moment there'd be a stampede that would turn the odds the other way. I never saw one.

Frank took care of the engineer and the fireman. Bill and I went for the express.

"Open up!" I yelled.

No answer.

"Bill, take some dynamite, and put it on the trucks and blow the damn' tightwad out."

"No, no! Don't do it! For God's sake, gentlemen. I'll open." The messenger pushed the door to, bowing and shaking, and invited us in as though it were his private den and we were about to have a finger and a smoke. The courtesy of express messengers at such times is a bit pathetic. This one had either thrown the key of the safe away or he had never had it.

The boodle was in a regular Wells Fargo steel chest. The lid closed over the top. I took a stick of dynamite, put it in the crack just under the lock.

The explosion sprung the sides and smashed the lock. There was $25,000 inside and not a note injured. We each drew $5,000 from that evening's pleasure.

I told the story to a quiet, homebody sort of woman once. Her eyes lit up with amazement and the keenest delight. That look gave me a large gob of joy. She wasn't so different from me, although she had never taken a cent in her life.

"You looked as if you wouldn't mind running your hand into a chest like that," I said.

"It's all in the point of view, at that," she answered.

Another time, a skilled musician, a respected citizen, the father of three chilldren, took me aside.

"On the level, did you get a rakeoff like that?" he wanted to know. "Well, what would it be worth to teach me the game?" I thought he was jesting until he had come three different times with the same proposition.

I didn't teach him. It is a game that always ends in a loss. The money goes. Happiness goes. Life goes.

Frank was the first to learn it. He turned the trick that sent us sneaking into Honduras in full dress suits and battered up hats.

He fell in love.

CHAPTER X

In the Panhandle; a starving hostess; theft and chivalry; $35,000 clear; dawning of romance; two plucky girls; the escape in the tramp.

We had been in the game nearly two years. Two hundred and some odd thousands had passed through our hands. It had passed quickly.

Our partnership was capitalized at $10,000 one particular evening when we struck across the panhandle of Texas after a hurried departure from New Mexico.

We had gone there on the trail of Houston and Love. We had never given up the hope of evening up our score with them. But by that time our business connections had become generally known. It became increasingly difficult to gain an entrée into any law-abiding city. Marshals in New Mexico fogged us a cargo of lead in the streets as a sort of salvo of welcome. We let it go as a farewell tribute and made a quick getaway.

The panhandle of Texas was forgotten of God Himself in those days. It was the bleakest, poorest, loneliest tongue of mesquite grass in all the Southwest. Deserted dugouts with their dingy chimneys sticking above the ground marked the spots where men had settled, struggled and failed.

The lobo wolves hid in the abandoned adobe holes. At the sound of the horses they would leap to the grass, their eyes, timid and frightened as a coyote's—one lope and they were gone. There was a breath of fear and desertion and unbearable quiet about those miles of prairie. It seemed isolated like an outlaw.

Perhaps that ride had something to do with quickening Frank's susceptibilities. For when we saw a ripple of smoke coming from a chimney about half a mile distant it seemed like a flag of life waving us back from a graveyard. Both of us laughed and spurred our horses to the dugout.

As we rode up a girl and a little fellow about five came out to meet us, as though they had expected our arrival. She was a tall, slender, bright-eyed bit of calico, with a kind of pathetic smile that went straight to Frank's heart. Her husband had gone to town a week before to buy the dinner, she said. He had forgotten to return.

Frank and I had not eaten for two days. Neither had the lady nor her little son. It was 12 miles to the nearest neighbor. I made the trip and brought back grub for the family. Frank and the girl were talking like old chums, the kid sitting on that train-robber's lap and running his small fingers over Frank's face in a trusting way that made my brother foolish with pride and happiness.

The lady cooked up the tastiest meal we had eaten in many months. She served with the grace of a duchess. Frank sat back and watched her, his eyes lighting with pleasure at every trifling word she said. This glimpse of home life was the first real adventure we had known in two years.

"The banker down there skinned that poor little

mite out of $5,000," Frank whispered to me. "Tricked her into signing some papers and then foreclosed on the mortgage. I'm going after the damn' thief and bring the boodle back to her."

The bank was in the little desert town in West Texas, where the husband had gone for provisions. We arrived there just before closing time the next day. With the help of our six-shooters in lieu of a checkbook we induced the cashier to turn over the lady's $5,000 and about $35,000 additional.

Idlers standing in the street, marshals and the sheriff made our exit difficult. They sent a hail of lead after us to coax the money back.

It would have been a brilliant getaway but for the lady's husband. He had been in town when the robbery was pulled off. As soon as he came to the dugout he sized us up and tipped off the posse. In the shooting that followed he was killed. We escaped, returned later and took the lady and her little fellow with us.

It was a long trip across Oklahoma and the Indian Territory into Arkansas. When it was over Frank was finished as far as our former business was concerned. He was in love with the girl. He could think of nothing else. For the first time he sat down to figure out the reasons that had made him turn bandit. He could not find any. He was full of self-reproach. He kept wondering why he had ever gone into the game and figuring out how long it would take him to get back.

"I'm going to quit." It did not surprise me.

"They won't let you quit," I warned him.

"Bunk," he answered; "nothing can stop me."

He was full of plans. We would go to New Orleans and then to the South Sea Islands. We had $35,000. It seemed enough to help us in jarring loose. I was ready for the adventure.

We did not know that at that very moment we had been tracked from West Texas on the bank-robbery almost to Fort Smith.

As soon as we stepped off the Mississippi packet to the levée in New Orleans a new life seemed to open for us. I felt free and cheerful as a good cow that has peacefully followed the herd and chewed in peace her daily cud. Our resolution to quit acted as a sort of absolution. We felt that we had cut loose from our past and that was the end of it.

Every incident in those first days enhanced this false sense of security. A few hours after we arrived I was browsing about the French quarter. A man passed, turned abruptly, came back and grabbed my arm. I thought I was caught. I jerked my six shooter and jammed it into his stomach, full cocked.

"God, Forney, don't you know me?"

When I saw little Ed——, my old pal at the Virginia Military Academy, shaking my hand, I'd have given the soul out of my body to have kept that forty-five out of sight. It was like a screaming voice telling him my brand, but it didn't seem to daunt him.

Ed was a sort of hero-worshiper. He liked me at college because I had been a cowpuncher. For much the same reason, outlawry seemed to him unusual and daring. With all the hospitality of the South, he invited me to visit his people.

They were wealthy. His father was a high official in Louisiana. While in his home we were almost certain of escape from detection. We went, Frank and I, and for weeks we lived in a fool's paradise. Life seemed an everlasting picture. We were home-hungry, and this visit was in the nature of a glorious new kind of spree—a sort of social intoxication.

Ed had a sister, Margaret. She was small and whimsical and black-eyed. I began to understand Frank's symptoms.

Summer in the South has many enchantments. I wanted to make this garden party perennial. Frank and I leased a steam yacht for a prolonged cruise in the gulf. Margaret, her mother, two cousins, Frank, Ed and I made up the party. There was a fine old family at Galveston, friends of Ed's family. We dropped anchor for a little visit with them.

And straightway they returned the compliment with a ball at the Beach Hotel. Of all my life that night was the happiest. Whatever Margaret saw in me I don't know. We were sitting in an alcove. Cape jasmines are fragrant in Galveston and the moon hung out like a big pearl. Music, soft and gentle, twined in with our thoughts. That kind of a night.

I hadn't heard any one come. A finger tapped me on the shoulder. I looked up.

"Step outside a moment," the man said.

"Take a look at me! Now, do you remember who I am? Well, I haven't forgotten what you did for me in El Reno. I'm going to square the debt."

The man had not taken his eyes from my face. I

knew him at once. I had saved him from the penitentiary when I was county attorney at El Reno. He was charged with the embezzlement of Wells Fargo funds. I was prosecutor. The man probably was guilty, but the evidence was entirely insufficient. The jury was prejudiced. I asked for a dismissal because it was the only square thing to do.

That was one loaf of bread on the waters that came back as cake.

"I'm with Wells Fargo," he whispered. "We have a bunch of dicks on the job. They know Al Jennings is in this hotel. The place is surrounded. I'm the only one who knows you by sight. Do the best you can."

I had not said a word. My heart was pounding like a triphammer. If I ever felt like pitying myself it was at that moment. The ignominy of it—the disgrace before these friends who honored us. I felt weak and limp all over. I went back to the alcove.

"What did he want, Al?" Margaret asked, her lips white and drawn. Before I could protest, she hurried on. "I know you are Al Jennings. I knew it all along. I knew you from the picture Ed has. What are you going to do?"

"Nothing. They won't get a chance."

The blunt way seemed best. I told her that Williams (that was the name Frank had taken; I was Edwards) was my brother; that we were wanted for a bank-robbery in West Texas; that our only chance was the Gulf of Mexico. She took it quiet and shrewd, without a whimper.

Frank was dancing with Margaret's cousin. We

waltzed over to them. I bumped against Frank.
"Look out," I warned. It was an old signal.
He followed us into the alcove.
"We're surrounded."
"Here? Oh, hell!"
Gardens that blossomed to the water's edge ran
in terraces about the hotel. We made our plan. Together, the four of us sauntered into a rose arbor,
laughing and talking as though our hearts were as
light as our tongues. The girls were as game as
veterans. They challenged us to a race. One lightning sprint and we were at the beach, the girls lag-
ging far behind.

Somebody's first-class dory helped our escape. It
was lying there with the oars set. Muscles of iron
sent that little yawl shooting across the water. The
gods of chance, $32,000 and our six-shooters were
with us. We didn't pause for breath until we
chopped against an old tramp banana steamer. We
clambered up the sides like aboriginal monkeys.

The captain was a smuggler of Three Star Hennessey brandy. When he saw two dudes in full-dress
suits, silk hats and white kid gloves tumbling over
his railing, he thought we were drunker than himself.
He wabbled up to us, his blowsy cheeks puffed out
like balloons, his pig eyes squinting and his addled
voice making a valiant attempt to order us off.

Put out tonight. No, sirs. Be damned and a
whole lot more if he would. He didn't have his
papers. He grew weepy over it. The government
wouldn't permit it.

When we slipped him $1,500, he changed his tune.

CHAPTER XI.

The meeting with O. Henry in Honduras; the celebration of the Fourth; quelling a revolution; a new flight; the girl on the beach.

A few hours later, Frank and I and our good friend, the smuggler, were plowing ahead under full steam for South America. I don't know to this day how long the trip lasted. Three Star Hennessey was rousing good company. We were so full of him, we didn't bother to find our bearings until one day the captain discovered his boat was out of water. At about the same time I began to thirst for a new drink. My throat was all but gutted with the smuggler's fiery brandy.

When the captain ordered his men into the yawl to bring back water in kegs, I went with them. About 200 yards from shore the water got so shallow we had to wade in.

My full-dress suit had lost one of its tails by this time; the white shirt was embossed with little hunks of dirt and splashes of whiskey. Only the rim of my stovepipe hat was left, an uncombed red mat stuck out through the ventilator.

With the water squashing about in my patent leather shoes, I was a queer looking pigwidgeon to strike up an acquaintance with the greatest men in Trojillo.

I wanted a drink and I wanted it quick. My tongue was hot and my feet were cold. I didn't have time to waste trying to make the natives of Honduras understand my perplexity. I caught sight of the American flag. In that parched and unslaked moment it meant the joy of freedom—liberty of the throat and the tongue.

Under the ripple of that flag I felt certain that I would find some kindred soul. I did.

On the porch of the squat wooden bungalow that housed the American consulate, sat an ample, dignified figure in immaculate white ducks. He had a large, nobly-set head, with hair the color of new rope and a full, straight-glancing gray eye that noted without a sparkle of laughter every detail of my ludicrous makeup.

He was already serene and comfortably situated with liquor, but he had about him an attitude of calm distinction. A rather pompous dignitary, he seemed to me, sitting there as though he owned the place. This, I thought, is indeed a man worthy to be the American consul.

I felt like a newsboy accosting a millionaire.

"Say, mister," I asked, "could you lead me to a drink? Burnt out on Three Star Hennessey. Got a different brand?"

"We have a lotion here that is guaranteed to uplift the spirit," he answered in a hushed undertone that seemed to charge his words with vast importance.

"Are you the American consul?" I ventured also in a whisper.

"No, just anchored here," he smuggled back the

information. Then his cool glance rested on the ragged edge of my coat.

"What caused you to leave in such a hurry?" he asked.

"Perhaps the same reason that routed yourself," I retorted.

The merest flicker of a smile touched his lips. He got up, took my arm and together we helped each other down the street, that was narrow as a burrow path, to the nearest cantina.

This was my first jaunt with William Sydney Porter. Together, we struck out on a long road that lost itself, for many years, in a dark tunnel. When the path broadened out again, it was the world's highway. The man at my side was no longer Bill Porter, the fugitive, the ex-convict. He was O. Henry, the greatest of America's short-story writers.

But, to me, in every detour of the road, he remained the same calm, whimsical Bill—baffling, reserved, loveable—who had led me to the Mexican doggery for my first drink in the paradise of fugitives.

In the dingy adobe estanca I found the solution guaranteed to uplift the spirit. But it was not in the sweet, heavy concoction the dignitary from the consulate called for. It was in the droll, unsmiling waggery of the conversation that came forth in measured, hesitant, excessively pure English as we leaned on the rickety wooden table and drank without counting our glasses.

Despite the air of distinction that was with him as a sort of birthmark, I felt at once drawn to him. I began to unfold my plan of settling in the country.

"This is an admirable location for a man who doesn't want much to do," he said.

"What line are you interested in?" I asked.

"I haven't given the matter much thought," he said. "I entertain the newcomers."

"You must be a hell of a busy man," I suggested.

"You're the first since my arrival."

He leaned over. "You probably wonder who I am and why I'm here?"

In Honduras every American is a subject of suspicion.

"Oh, God, no," I put in quickly. "In my country nobody asks a man's name or his past. You're all right."

"Thanks, colonel." He drew in his upper lip in a manner that was characteristic. "You might call me Bill. I think I would like that."

Several hours we sat there, an ex-highwayman in a tattered dress suit and a fugitive in spotless white ducks, together planning a suitable investment for my stolen funds. Porter suggested a cocoanut plantation, a campaign for the presidency, an indigo concession.

There was something so fascinating in the odd surprise lurking in his remarks, I found myself waiting for his conclusions. I forgot that the *Helena* had but stopped for water and might even now be well cleared of the shores of Honduras.

The mate beckoned to me. I nearly knocked the table over in my haste.

"Just a moment." Porter's unruffled undertone held me as though he had put a restraining hand on my arm. "You are an American. Have you considered the celebration of the glorious Fourth?"

"Fourth, what?"

"The Fourth of July, colonel, which falls at one minute past 12 tonight. Let us have some festivity on the occasion."

Every one who knows O. Henry knows how three loyal prodigals celebrated the nation's birth. He has made it memorable in his story, "The Fourth in Salvador." What he couldn't remember he fabricated, but many of the details, with the exception of the ice plant and the $1,000 bonus from the government, happened just as he has narrated them.

Somehow we got Frank off the boat. Long after midnight Porter took us to the consulate, where he made his home. He had a little cot in one corner of the main room. He took the blankets from it and spread them on the floor. The three of us stretched out.

About 11 o'clock in the morning the celebration of the Fourth opened. Porter, Frank, two Irishmen who owned an indigo concession, the American consul, myself and a negro, brought along for the sake of democracy, made up the party. For a fitting observance of America's triumph Porter insisted that the English consul join us. We put the matter before his majesty's subject. He agreed that it would be a "devil of a fine joke."

There were but four life-size houses in Trojillc. Under the shade of the governor's mansion we stood and sang "The Star Spangled Banner." Out of deference to our guest Porter suggested that we render one verse of "God Save the King." The Britisher objected. "Don't make damn' nonsense of this occasion," he demurred.

We started out to shoot up the town in true Texas style, prepared to wind up the fireworks with a barbecued goat in the lemon grove near the beach. We never got to the barbecue. A revolution intervened.

We had shot up two estancas. Glass was shattered everywhere. The Carib barkeepers had fled. We were helping ourselves and scrupulously laying the money for every drink on the counter.

Suddenly a shot was fired from the outside. Porter had just finished smashing up a mirror with a bottle. He turned with a quiet that was as ludicrous as it was inimitable.

"Gentlemen," he said, "the natives are trying to steal our copyrighted Fourth."

We made a clattering dash for the street, shooting wildly into the air. A little man in a flaming red coat came galloping by. About 30 barefoot horsemen, all in red coats and very little else, tore up a mighty cloud of dust in his wake. They fired off their old-fashioned muzzle loaders as if they really meant murder.

As the leader whirled past on his diminutive gray pony Porter caught him by the waist and dragged him off. I sprang into the saddle, shooting and yelling like a maniac.

"Reinforcements, reinforcements!" Like a song of victory the shout thundered from the rear. I don't know where or how I rode.

But the next day the governor and two of his little

tan Caribs called at the consulate. He wished to thank the American patriots for the magnificent aid they had given in quelling the revolution. They had saved the republic! With a lordly air he offered us the cocoanut plantations that grew wild all over the country. The incredible daring of the American riders had saved the nation!

We didn't even know there had been a revolution. And we didn't know whose side we had taken. Porter rose to the occasion.

"We appreciate the government's attitude," he answered, with a touch of patronage in his tone. "So often patriots are forgotten."

It seems that in that moment when we rushed wildly to the door of the cantina we changed the tide of battle. The government troops were chasing the rebels and the rebels were winning. We had rallied the royal army and led it to victory. It was a bloodless battle.

Our triumph was short-lived. The government and the rebel leaders patched up their differences. The rebel general demanded amends for the insult to his troops. He demanded the lives of the outsiders who had impudently ended a revolution before it had decently begun.

The American consul advised a hasty and instant departure.

"Is there no protection in this realm for an American citizen?" I asked.

"Yes," Porter declared. "The State Department will refer our case to Mark Hanna. He will investigate our party affiliations. It will then be referred to the bureau of immigration, and by that time **we** will all be shot."

Flight was our only recourse. We started toward the beach. As we ran a little Carib girl about 15 came scooting out from a hedge and hurled herself against me. She was crying and talking and clutching my arm. I couldn't understand a word she was saying. Porter tried a little Spanish.

"The little girl is in great distress," he said. "She is saying something entirely beyond my comprehension of the Spanish language. I gather that she wants to be one of our party."

Scarcely were the words out of her mouth when a burly fellow much bigger than the natives broke through the hedge and grabbed the tiny creature by the hair. It interrupted our conversation. I landed him a smash on the head with my 45 gun.

Just then a signal rang out. It was the call to arms. The army was after us.

Porter, Frank and I, with the little maid at our heels, made for the beach. Porter stopped a moment to ask the little Carib, in the gravest English, her pardon for his haste. He had a most pressing engagement, he said, some 2,000 miles away. She was not satisfied and stood shrieking on the beach while we rowed out to the *Helena*.

It bothered Porter. Years afterward, when we were together in New York, he recalled the incident.

"Remember that little strip of brown muslin that fluttered down the street after us in Trojillo? I wondered what she was saying."

He didn't like "unfinished stories."

Bill, the newfound friend, had thrown in his lot with us. He didn't have a cent in the world. He didn't know where we were going or who we were.

"What is your destination?" he asked quietly, as the *Helena* steamed up.

"I left America to avoid my destination," I told him.

"How far can you go?"

"As far as $30,000 will take us."

It took us farther than we reckoned.

CHAPTER XII.

Voyaging at leisure; the grand ball in Mexico City; O. Henry's gallantry; the don's rage; O. Henry saved from the Spaniard's knife.

Like aimless drifters in a boat that has neither rudder nor compass, we started on that tour of investigation. We planned to loll along, stopping as we would, looking for a pleasant soil in which to plant ourselves. But we made not the slightest effort to map our course.

And then suddenly, across that idle way, there rippled a little stick of chance, an incident so trivial and insignificant we scarcely noticed it. In a moment it had broken the waters and our boat was all but wrecked by the unconsidered wisp. Bill Porter nearly lost his life for a smile!

The captain of the *Helena* was at our service. We stopped at Buenos Aires and rode out through the pampas country, but it did not attract us.

Peru was no more alluring. We were looking for big game. And the mighty pastime of this realm was the shooting of the Asiatic rats that stampeded the wharves.

For no particular reason, two of us being acknowledged fugitives and the third a somewhat mysterious soldier of fortune, we stopped off at Mexico City. We knew Porter only as Bill. I had told him the main facts of my life. He did not return the confidence and we did not seek it. Neither Frank nor I placed him in our own class. He was secretive, but we did not attribute the trait to any sinister cause. With the romance of the cowpuncher I figured that this fine, companionable fellow was troubled with an unhappy love affair.

We had loafed along, deliberately dodging issues. At the Hotel De Republic fate turned the little trick that compelled us to change our course.

I was sitting in the lobby waiting for Frank and Porter. Something like a clutch on my arm struck through my listlessness. It was a breath-taking moment. I felt a presence near. I feared to look up. Then a gigantic hand reached down to me. Jumbo Rector, idol of cadet days in Virginia, had picked me to my feet.

Rector was six feet six. I reached a bit above his elbow. We had been the long and the short of it in every devilment pulled in college. If there was one man on the earth I was glad to see at that moment it was this buoyant, healthy-hearted Samson.

Rector had built the Isthmian railroad. He had a palace of white stone and he brought us bag and baggage to his hacienda. That night I told him the things that had happened in the 16 years since we parted.

"Who is this friend of yours, this Bill?" he asked me later. "Are you sure of him? He looks to me like a detective."

"I don't like your friend Rector," Porter confided the same night. "He has a most unpleasant way of scrutinizing one."

Not many days later both Porter and I had proof of Rector's worth. The antipathy between the two was but superficial. There was to be a grand ball at the hotel. All the notables, Porfirio Diaz, the cabinet, the señoritas and the dons were to be present. Rector had us all invited.

We went through preparations as elaborate as a débutante's. Rector loaned us his tailor, and the three of us were outfitted in faultless evening attire. As we were dressing I slipped on my shoulder scabbard. Frank and Rector ridiculed me.

"Let him wear his side arms," Porter jibed. "There should be one gentleman in the party."

"I guarantee you won't need them tonight," Rector promised.

I took them off, but reluctantly. I came back later and slipped the six-shooter into my trousers' belt. That precaution saved the "Four Million" and all her treasured successors for America.

Porter looked a prince that night. Always fastidious about his person, the full dress enhanced his air of distinction. He was a figure to arrest attention in any gathering.

And he was in one of his most inconsequent, bantering moods. We stood against the column commenting on the dress of the dons and the Americans. The Spaniards, in their silk stockings and the gay-colored sashes about their slick-fitting suits, seemed to Porter to harmonize with the beauty and the music of the scene.

"These people have poetry in their make-up," he said. "What an interesting spectacle they make.

As if to illustrate his words, the handsomest couple on the floor swung past. If ever there was a flawless job turned out by God it was that Spanish don. There were a hundred years of culture behind the charm in his manner; the grace in his walk. He was slimly made, quick and elegant. He had a face of chisled perfection.

The don's partner was a girl of most extraordinary beauty—unusual and compelling. Her red hair, her magnificent blue eyes and her pearl-white skin stood out, among so many dark faces, as something touched with an unnatural radiance. She wore a lavender gown. She had the color and the witchery of a living opal.

I turned to call Bill's attention. The girl had noticed him. As she passed she gave the faintest toss of her head and a smile that was more in the tail of her eye than on her lip. With the deference due to a queen, Porter smiled and made a courtly bow. The don stiffened, but not a muscle of his handsome face twitched. I knew that the incident was not closed.

"Bill, you're making a mistake. You're breeding trouble among these people," I told him.

"Colonel, I feel that that would enliven the occasion." The imperturable, hushed tone gave no indication of the reckless devilment of his mood. Porter was as full of whims as an egg is of meat.

"Sir, I see that you are a stranger here," a voice that was mellow as thick cream addressed us. It was the don. His smile would have been a warning to any man but Bill Porter. "You are not accustomed to our ways. I regret that I have not the honor of your acquaintance. Had I that honor I should be glad to introduce you to the señorita. Since I cannot claim the privilege, I beg you to desist in your attentions to my affianced."

The English was perfect. The don bowed and walked leisurely off. His flow of gentility won me. I could not help comparing him to the money-grabbing, flat-footed boors that decorate an American ballroom. The Castilian seemed to me worthy of respect. Porter was not at all impressed by his request.

The grand march passed again. I do not know what devilment possessed the girl. It seemed to run like an electric current from her to Porter. As she stepped toward him she dropped her mantilla—so lightly, so deftly, that it did not even arrest the attenion of the don.

Porter stooped down, picked it up, held it a moment and then passed behind the couple. He flashed a glance of joyous chivalry at the señorita, bowed and handed the lace directly to her.

"Señorita, you dropped this, did you not?" he said. She took it and smiled. Never was Bill Porter more magnetic than that night.

"Now you've played hell," I said. He had committed a mortal breach, and he knew it. Spanish etiquette demanded that the presentation be made to the don, who would thank him for the señorita.

"I've played everything else," he answered undisturbed. The incident had passed. It was at least 10 minutes later. Neither of us saw the don coming until he stood like a tiger before Porter. With a sweep that was lightning, he brought his open hand down in a ringing blow full across Porter's face.

The blow was so sudden, so full of swift animal fury, it knocked Porter against the column. The don drew back, brushing his hand in scornful contempt. The by-standers stood aghast at the stinging humiliation of the patrician stranger.

It was but the breath of an instant. Porter leaped up, his broad shoulders hunched forward, his face crimson with rage. On his cheek, four livid welts stood out like white blisters. In that scene of exquisite culture, the ferocity of the jungle was unleashed.

Like a mad bull, Porter sprang for the don, striking right and left.

The don hurled himself forward, gripping Porter about the waist. Something flashed. The next second, his stiletto was driving straight for Porter's throat.

It was Bill's life or the don's.

I fired in the Spaniard's face.

The sudden roar went like dynamite through the ballroom. The don fell, Porter stood as though hewn of stone, a look of white horror frozen to his face. From everywhere voices whispered and all at once raised into a mighty protest.

Out from the corridors two men dashed the crowd aside, charging upon us. Rector swept me into his gigantic arms as though I were a kitten. Frank caught Porter and pushed him hurriedly from the room.

Rector's carriage stood waiting. We were hustled

into it. The most dismal ride of my life began. Not a word was said. Porter sat like a man stricken cold with staggering dismay.

Frank slumped down in one corner, sullen with anger, recoiling from me as though I had done an evil thing. It lashed me as a torment. I felt their tense nervousness, but I felt justified as well.

I had not killed deliberately. I had acted only to save Bill. The death of the don did not trouble me. Porter's quiet stung like a wasp bite. I wanted someone to tell me I had done the right thing.

Resentment and an unbearable irritation against all of them bit into me. I felt as though I were in the "Black Maria" on the way to the scaffold. An oppressive hush weighed like a suffocating hot breath upon us.

The carriage swung through a narrow lane of palms. The trees looked like upraised black swords. The monotonous clatter of the hoofbeats was the only sound. The silence seemed an intentional reproach to me.

"Damned ingratitude"—I hissed out the words more to myself than to them. Porter stirred and leaned forward. His hand went out and caught mine. I felt immediately at peace. No word could have filled me with the satisfaction of that warm, expressive clasp.

For miles we rode silently, swiftly. Not a comment! Rector lit a cigar. In the soft match-light, I caught a glimpse of Porter's face.

It was still struck with that shocked look of repugnance as though he were recoiling from himself and the thoughtless caprice that had precipitated the ugly tragedy. It was such an unfair consequence of that moment of bantering gaiety.

In a mood of unwonted levity he had answered the challenge in a smile. It was an ordinary ballroom episode. And for that pleasantry he was crushed down with this overwhelming disaster.

The big misfortunes of his life seem all to have come upon him with as little invitation. The law of cause and effect in his case worked in an inscrutable fashion.

When Porter put out his hand to me the tragedy was over as far as I was concerned. To him it was always a hideous memory.

Once he alluded to it. We were sitting together in the warden's office in the Ohio penitentiary.

"That night," he said, "was the most terrible in my life." I could not understand. That the don should die if Porter were to live seemed clearly inevitable.

"Why?" I asked.

"Colonel, I was as guilty as a murderer," he said.

"You're not sorry it was the don who went down?" His version stung me.

"I've always regretted it," he answered.

His regret was not for the don's death so much as for the failure of his own life. I think that many times Porter would have welcomed death to the galling humiliation of prison life.

If we could have stayed in Mexico all of us might have escaped the shadows of unhappy pasts. We were hurried out and none of us wished to leave.

Down toward the peninsula, about 50 miles south-west of Mexico City, the richest valley in the world lay. We had looked it over.

It was to have been our home. Things grew there almost spontaneously. Bananas, corn, alligator pears asked only to be planted. The palms were magnificent.

"Here," Porter said when we had decided to purchase it, "one could work and dream out his imagery." I did not know what he meant. I learned when I read "Cabbages and Kings." Here, too, Frank and I hoped to reëstablish ourselves. Each had his own dream.

In that silent ride the vision passed. To Frank and to me it was but another misadventure in lives already overcrowded. Neither of us realized that a bitter crisis had been reached in the life of the reti-cent, droll-tongued fellow, "Bill."

We never dreamed that prison waited for him as it did for us. We never thought that this born aris-tocrat would one day be compelled to eat at a "hog trough" with thieves and murderers and to bend his pride to the ignorant scowl of a convict guard. Por-ter, I think, knew that the die was cast for him when we left Mexico.

If we could have planted ourselves in that miracu-lous valley he might have escaped the forbidding future awaiting him. He could have sent for his daughter. He would have avoided the shame of that striped suit—the shame that wore into his heart and broke his life up in wretchedness.

But he smiled lightly at the don's señorita, and

consequences hurled him back to face the issues he had dodged.

It is easy now to understand the look of rigid horror on his face as we got down at Rector's home.

Jumbo poured whiskey for us and tried to lighten our mood. Porter was so unstrung that when the coachman knocked to tell us the team was ready he reeled and seemed about to collapse.

"Don't worry," Rector said as he shook hands. "Everything will be all right. You can trust this driver. I'm going back to the hotel. I will tell the officers you are at my home. It will give you a fair start."

We went to a little way station on the Tampico road, later caught a tramp steamer at Mazatlan and finally arrived at San Diego, striking out on a flying trip to San Francisco. We never got there.

CHAPTER XIII.

In California; the bank-robbery; O. Henry's refusal; purchase of a ranch; coming of the marshals; flight and pursuit; the trap; capture at last.

O. Henry has been called a democrat, a citizen of the world. The laboratory wherein he caught and dissected the hearts of men and women was in the alleys and honkatonks. He sought to interpret life in the raw, not in the superficial livery disguising it on the broad ways. The under dog was his subject But at heart he was an aristocrat.

He had all the proud sensitiveness of the typical Southern gentleman. He liked to mingle with the masses; he was not one of them. Gladly he threw in his lot with a pair of bandits and fugitives. It would have cut him to the soul to have been branded as one of them.

For his haughty nature, the ramble from Mexico to San Diego and up the coast to San Francisco was fraught with disagreeable suspense. It was humiliating to "be on the dodge."

I will never forget the look of chagrin that spread over his face when I bumped against him and Frank just as the ferry boat was swinging into the slip.

"Sneak," I said. "They're here."

The chief of the Wells Fargo detectives was on the boat. He had brushed against my arm. Before he had an opportunity to renew old acquaintance, I sauntered over to Frank and Porter. Wells Fargo had many uncollected claims against me. I was not ready for the settlement. Captain Dodge was probably unaware of my presence. We could not afford to take any chances. We stayed on the boat and it brought us back to Oakland.

Bill was a trifle upset. He insisted on staking us all to a drink, although he had to borrow the money from me to pay for the treat. Texas seemed to be the only safe camping ground for us.

With about $417 left from our capital of $30,000, we landed in San Antonio, still hankering for the joys of simple range life. There I met an old cowman friend of mine and he took us out to his ranch. Fifty miles from the town it ran into low hills and valleys, prairies and timber. A finer strip of country no peeler would ask. The cowman offered us range, cattle and horses for $15,000.

It was a bargain. Frank and I decided to snap it up. Financial arrangements, the cowman assured us, could be made with the bank in ———— ————, several hundred miles distant. In the safe there was at least $15,000, and it could be easily removed. This was a straight tip.

It was a peculiar situation. Frank and I had both decided to quit the outlaw life. But we hadn't a cent and there was but one way to gather a quick haul. The fine fervor of reformation had lost its early ardor. Necessity completed the cooling process.

But we were a little worried about Porter. Whatever may have been his reasons for staying with us we were confident that Bill was not a lawbreaker.

The very thing that decided us to take him into our confidence was his pride. We knew he needed the money. We knew it humiliated him to borrow.

I had given him many and various sums since our flight from Honduras. These were always accepted as loans. We didn't want Bill to be under an obligation to us. We wanted him to earn his interest in the ranch.

The square thing was to invite him to go into the banking venture. If you had seen Bill Porter's face then and the helpless surprise that scooted across it, you would believe as I do that he was never guilty of the theft which sent him for nearly four years of his life to the Ohio Penitentiary. He had neither recklessness nor the sangfroid of the lawbreaker.

Just about evening I went down to the corral. Porter was sitting there enjoying the quiet peace. He was rolling a corn-shuck cigarette.

He looked happier and more at ease than at any time since the shooting of the don. I suppose I should have broached the subject mildly. The satisfying dreariness of this October night was not suggestive of crime or robbery. But the gentleness of the Madonna would not have lured Bill Porter into the scheme.

"Bill," I said, "we're going to buy the ranch for $15,000 and we want you to come in with us on the deal."

He paused with his cigarette half rolled.

"Colonel," he said, "I would like nothing better than to settle in this magnificent country, and to live here unafraid and unmolested. But I have no funds."

"That's just it. Neither have we. We're about to get them. Down there in ———, there's a bank with $15,000 in its vaults. That money ought to be put into circulation."

The tobacco dropped from the paper. Porter looked up quickly and searched my face. He saw that I was in earnest. He was not with us, but not for a fortune would he wound us or even permit me to think that he judged us.

"Colonel—" This time his large eyes twinkled. It was seldom that he smiled. I never heard him laugh but twice. "I'd like a share in this range. But tell me, would I have to shoot anybody?"

"Oh, perhaps so, but most likely not."

"Well, give me the gun. If I go on the job I want to act like an expert. I'll practice shooting."

No outlaw would ever ask another for his forty-five. The greatest compliment a cowpuncher can give the man he trusts is to hand over his gun for inspection.

Porter took the honor lightly. He handled the gun as though it were a live scorpion. I forgot to warn him that I had removed the trigger and the gun would not stay cocked. By this device I could shoot faster at close range, gaining a speed almost equal to the modern automatic.

Like all amateurs, Bill put his thumb on the hammer and pulled it back. Then he started walking back and forth with the forty-five in his hand and his hand dropped to his side. Without intending to, he shifted his grip, releasing his thumb from the hammer.

There was a sudden, sharp explosion, a little geyser of earth spurted upward. When it cleared there was a hole as big as a cow's head scooped in the ground. My forty-five lay in the depression. Porter, scared but unhurt, stood staring over it.

"Colonel," he looked up at me a little abashed, "I think I would be a hindrance on this financial undertaking."

I wanted Porter to go with us. We didn't need him, but I had already grown very fond of the moody, reticent, cultured fellow. I didn't want him to be dependent on us and I wanted his company on the range.

"Well, you needn't take the gun. You just stay outside and hold the horses. We really need you for that.

He hesitated a moment.

"I don't believe I could even hold the horses," he answered.

Troubled and fearful lest we should never return, he bade us good-bye. I did not know until the deal was closed and the ranch ours, the days of worry and misery that Bill Porter suffered while Frank and I went down to take up the matter with the bank.

We left Porter, harried with anxiety, at the Hotel Plaza in San Antonio. Frank and I and the rancher rode into ———.

Our plan was simple. The cowman was to attract the attention of the marshals while we cleaned out the bank's vault.

The bank stood on a corner opposite the public square. The cowman went quietly to a bench to wait for the signal from me. I pulled out my handkerchief and began mopping my face. He opened fire, shooting like a lunatic into the air. Men and women ran into the saloons, stores, houses. The officials hurried over to the crazy cowman.

Frank and I walked into the bank, stuck up the cashier and compelled the delivery of $15,560 in currency. The rancher, charged with drunkenness, was arrested, fined and released. Frank and I left the bank as quietly as the next-door merchant might have. The ruse worked.

We went straight to the ranch and then doubled back to San Antonio. It was about two days since we had left Porter. He was not ordinarily a warmspoken man, but when he saw us he put out his hand and his voice was rich with suppressed emotion.

"Colonel, congratulations. This is indeed a happy moment. I was so troubled in your absence." From Bill Porter that greeting was more expressive than the gustiest tribute from the glib-tongued. Porter's stories are crowded with colorful slang. His own speech was invariably pure and correct.

All of us knew that the parting had come. If Bill could not rob with us he could not settle down on the range bought with our stolen bills.

I have never relished farewells. I did not want to probe into Porter's soul. He had never said a word about his past. He had not even told us his name. But little as I wished to quiz him, I was eager to know his identity. I did not want to lose track of him forever.

"Bill," I said, "here's where we split out. We're getting on mighty familiar soil. There's likely to be trouble enough some day. Something may turn up.

I'd like to write to you. I might want your advice."

"I haven't been very frank with you, have I?" he answered. "I'm sorry."

Such reticence, I felt, was more than a shield for an unhappy love-affair. Porter's troubles, I knew, must be deeper than I had suspected.

"Good-bye, colonel; may we meet happily again," he said.

And the next time I saw him, nearly three years later, the very word "happy" was stricken from his vocabulary.

Frank and I went out to our ranch. For six months we lived in free and profitable industry. Suddenly an old, familiar face peered in at our window. "Mex," a bandit friend, had tracked our haunt. Other faces appeared on the range and dodged again. The marshals had located us.

Frank, Mex and I escaped. For weeks we rode from range to range. Hunger spurred us. There were more robberies. And then there was the Rock Island daylight holdup. We had counted on a clean haul of $90,000 from the express car. Our dynamite failed to break the safe. We were cheated on the transaction.

It was our most futile venture. It led to our capture. The stickup was counted the boldest in outlaw exploits. Armed bands patrolled the country for the "Jennings gang." In December, '97, they caught us.

We had gone back to the old Spike S, the range where I had first met and joined the outlaws, the range where the M., K. and T. robbery was planned. We were waiting the arrival of "Little Dick."

There came a knock at the door. The wind was howling like a fiend outside. Mrs. Harliss went to the porch. A man, covered with dirt, his eyes swollen almost shut, his coat dripping with rain, asked shelter. He was a ranchman who lived some miles away. That night he came as a spy. We were his quarry.

All of us felt the "closing of the trap." We had nothing but our suspicions to work on. The rancher was a friend of the Harliss folk. We could not hold him.

But none of us went to bed that night.

The sun came blazing out brilliant but cold the next morning. Mrs. Harliss went down to the cistern for water. She came rushing back, her shawl gone, her hair blowing in the wind.

"The marshals are here! We'll all be killed!"

Frank and Bud hurled themselves downstairs, Winchesters in their hands. Mrs. Harliss grabbed her little brother in her arms and ran to the front door. I started out through the kitchen window.

Bullets tore the knobs off the front door. The first volley splintered glass in my face. We got to a little box-house just outside the ranch home. There were three rooms downstairs, one up. The shots went through the house as though it were cardboard.

Bullets broke the dishes on the table, smashed the stove, dashed the pictures off the wall. Three of us were hit. We were surrounded on three sides. Marshals were in the barn to the northeast, the log house to the north and the rocks and timber to the northwest; a little peach orchard skirted the south. Beyond that was open prairie.

We fought for 40 minutes, until our rickety fortress was all but shattered. Then we hit for the prairie, firing as we ran. They didn't dare to track us into the open spaces.

Just across the Duck Creek we stopped to bind our wounds. I was shot above the knee, the bullet lodging in the bone. Bud was shot in the shoulder, and Bill had a gash that looked like a dog bite in his thigh. Frank's clothes had 27 holes in the coat. He was not even scratched.

Up in the mountains we prepared for a "last stand." We hid all day. It was blue cold. Between us we had two apples. That was our fare for three days. The marshals didn't follow.

We recrossed the creek, took a couple of Indians and their pony team prisoners and made for the Canadian River bed. My wound swelled. I had to rip it open twice with my penknife to get relief. We made straight for Benny Price's house. He had been a friend of ours before the outlaw days. He took us in and gave us a good meal. We could not stay without menacing his welfare.

There was another friend there, a horsethief named Baker. He came down and gave us a wagon. Frank did not trust him. He would not go. Bud, Bill and I got into the covered wagon. Baker was to drive us to his house. Bill seemed to be dying with his wounds. Bud and I were both unconscious. I came to. Someone was sitting on the driver's seat.

"Who is it?" I asked.

"Me, damn it!" Frank answered. "Let's get out of this."

While we were unconscious, Baker sent word to Frank that I wanted him. He had come. Baker drove us into the timber, into the trap, and left us vowing that we were on the right road. A felled tree lay athwart the path. Bill was dying. Bud and I, but half conscious, were dozing in the bottom of the wagon. Frank had scrambled out to move the tree.

The cordon of marshals, six-shooters cocked, sprang about us.

"Jennings, surrender!"

About ten to one, they had us.

It took nearly two years before sentence was passed. I was given five years on a charge of assault with intent to kill a deputy. In another district I was found guilty of the Rock Island holdup and given life imprisonment. I was sent to the Ohio penitentiary.

The mystery of fate had brought me to the home of Bill Porter.

CHAPTER XIV.

In prison men live unnatural lives. Brutal associations are forced upon them. They are fed at a hog trough, locked into stifling cells and denied all wholesome communication with right-living people. The devices employed to crush out the better instincts are monstrous beyond the conception of healthy-minded men and women.

The confinement cramps and yellows even the city man. The outlaw, used to the big freedom of the plains and the mountains, is a doomed man once he steps inside the gray stone walls.

As soon as I felt the heavy breath of the prison—the breath laden with evil smells, charged with bitter curses, pulsing with hushed resentment—the beast reared within me.

My arrival had been heralded by every newspaper in the State. Every man in the prison knew it. Two train-robbers, former friends of mine on the outside, wanted to renew old acquaintance. By some crook, they managed to pass me in the corridor.

They were as ghosts. For a moment I could not recall them. Like white shadows, long and bent, they glided past. One year in the penitentiary had evaporated the life from their bodies. They came in husky giants. They went out wasted wrecks.

And then there was my first meal. The odor of slumgullion, of putrid meat, of millions of flies, surged in an overpowering wave upon me as the door of the dining-room opened. I sat on a stool between two sweaty negroes, who were more like gorillas than men.

There was the clatter of tin, the shuffle of uneasy feet, the waving of upraised hands signaling the guards for bread. No sound of the human voice, but that God-forsaken, weighty, brutal dumbness imposed upon convicts in the penitentiary.

At each place there was a tin of stew. Maggots floated in the gravy. A hunk of bread and a saucer of molasses and flies filled out the ménu. I had been used to coarse fare. This stinking filth sickened me.

A burly, red-faced fellow opposite leaned over, his face almost in his plate, and shoveled in the noisome stew. He raised two fingers. A trusty came down, a great dishpan hung from his neck. With one swipe he ladled out a scoop of the foul mess and splattered it on the red fellow's plate.

Every time the guards helped a prisoner they whacked the food down so that bits of the meat or fluid spattered. Some of the gravy splashed across the narrow board and slopped in my face. In an instant I was on my feet. The negro at my side pulled me down.

"Doan want yoah 'lasses?" he asked. I pushed it over to him.

He put in his thumb, jabbed out the flies, smudged them on the table, and ate.

Shoved into the cell for the night, I felt that I was forgotten by all the world. The cell was in reality a stone vault, four by eight feet. It had no window. The only ventilation came from the barred door that opened on the closed corridor. There were two straw ticks on wooden shelves. These were the bunks. Another man shared the fetid hole with me.

The cells were entirely without sanitary equipment. On Saturday night the men were locked up and kept in this stifling confinement until Monday morning. Two men sleeping, breathing, tramping about in a walled space four by eight for 36 hours turned that closet into a hell. It was no longer air that filled the place, but a reeking stench.

When the first Monday morning came I decided to move. I had been placed in the transfer office. Few prisoners are qualified to act as clerks. I was given this office position the day after my arrival. It was my business to keep a check on all the men, to tabulate all transfers from one cell to another and to check up on all releases. Not an official nor a clerk could leave the prison until every convict was accounted for.

There was one cell block called the "Bankers' Row." It was fitted up for the privileged convicts. These high financiers were gentlemen. They had not held up trains and, at the risk of life and limb, robbed the State of $20,000 or $40,000.

They had sat in well-furnished offices and lolled in easy chairs while they did their thieving. They

were polite about it when they filched the funds
entrusted to them by laborers, small investors, working girls.

They ground hundreds of struggling families under heel, but they were careful to conceal the blood
stains. They had pilfered in millions.

They were entitled to consideration. They got it.

Cells in Bankers' Row were neat parlors compared
to the vaults in the I. N. K. block, where I was
settled. They had mirrors, a curtain on the door and
a carpet on the floor. One of the exclusive convicts
was discharged. I transferred myself into his cell.

When I appeared in the select promenade in the
morning my hickory shirt called for comment. The
bankers were all prison clerks. They were permitted
to wear white shirts. An elegant, pursy-faced, corpulent bundle of Southern gentility accosted me.
His bank had "failed" for $2,000,000.

"Good morning, sah. You are a banker, I presume?"

"Yes," I answered.

"National?" He was merely interested in a col-
league.

"Not particularly. I robbed any and all of them.
You are an embezzler?"

The magnate from New Orleans spluttered out
his surprised disgust. His neat face was crimson
with resentment.

"I am heah."

"Yes, sah; so am I," I answered.

"I think there must be a mistake." He walked
off haughtily.

"So do I. I am going back with the horse-thieves, where I'll be among gentlemen."

My departure was more precipitous than I had planned. A jealous convict "snitched." The deputy warden sent for me.

"Who transferred you?" he asked.

"The transfer clerk," I answered. Lucky for me the deputy was in a good humor.

"What for?"

"A good bed, a carpet, some clean air."

"Those rooms are for bankers," he informed me.

"I'm a banker."

"Not their sort. They didn't terrify with a gun. You go back to your own range. They might steal what you've got."

So I went back to my hole. I had grown used to prison bread. I learned how to skim the worms out of the stew. I could do without molasses. But I could not endure the Sundays. They left me weak, stifled, murderous. The fourth one since my arrival dawned.

Every Sunday in the Ohio penitentiary an attendant from the hospital visited the cells dispensing pills and quinine. The allotment was always given to the prisoners whether they needed them or not.

The hospital attendant was standing at my door. I felt his glance, but I did not meet it. And then a voice, hushed and measured, that to me seemed like sunlight breaking through a cloud, sounded in my ear.

The low rich tones rippled through the black prison

curtain. The waving prairies and the soft hills of the Texas ranch; the squat bungalow at Honduras, the tropical valley of Mexico; the magnificent scene in the ballroom was before me.

"Colonel, we meet again."

In all my life there has never been a tenser moment than when Bill Porter spoke that simple greeting. It caught me like a stab in the heart. I felt like crying. I could not bear to look him in the face.

I did not want to see Bill Porter in convict stripes. For months we shared the same purse, the same bread, the same glass. We had traveled through South America and Mexico together. Not a word had he said of his past. And here it was torn open for me to see and the secret he had kept so quietly shouted out in his gray, prison suit with the black band running down the trousers. The proudest man I have ever known was standing outside a barred door, dispensing quinine and pills to jailbirds.

"Colonel, we have the same tailor, but he does not provide us with the same cut of clothes," the old droll, whimsical voice drawled without a chuckle. I looked into the face that would have scorned to show its emotion. It was still touched with grave, impressive hauteur, but the clear eyes, in that moment, seemed filmed and hurt.

I think it was about the only time in my life I did not feel like talking. Bill was looking at my ill-fitting hand-me-downs. I had received the castoff clothes of some other prisoner. They hung on me like the flapping rags on a scarecrow. The sleeves were rolled up and the trousers tucked back. My shoes were four sizes too large. When I walked, it sounded like the clatter of a horse brigade.

"But you'll soon be promoted to the first rank," Porter said. He had deliberately sought the task of dispensing the pills in order to get me a word of advice.

"Colonel—" He spoke quickly. Conversation was forbidden. The guard might come into the range at any moment. "Be careful of the friends you choose. On the outside it may be safe to pick up acquaintances at every siding. I'm glad you were sociably inclined at Honduras. The O. P. is a different country. Have no confidants."

It was valuable advice. I would have escaped six months of torture in solitary confinement had I heeded it.

"And when you graduate into the first grade, I'll see what 'pull' can do for you. There may be a chance to have you transferred to the hospital."

That was all. The stealthy footfall of the guard brushed along the corridor. We looked at each other a moment. Porter flipped a few pills into my hand and carelessly walked off.

As he left, the utter isolation of the prison was intensified. The cell walls seemed heaving together, closing me into a black pit. I felt that I would never see Bill Porter again.

He had said nothing of himself. I knew that he was convicted on a charge of embezzlement. I never asked him about it. One day in New York, years later, he alluded to it. He was shaving in his room in the Caledonia Hotel. We were talking of old times in the Ohio penitentiary. He wanted me to tell him of a bank-robbery we had pulled in the outlaw days.

"Bill, what did you fall for?" I asked. He turned upon me a look of quizzical humor, rubbed the lather into his chin, and waited a moment before he answered.

"Colonel, I have been expecting that question, lo, these many years. I borrowed four from the bank on a tip that cotton would go up. It went down, and I got five."

It was but another of his quips. Porter, I believe, and all of his friends share the confidence, was innocent of the charge laid against him. He was accused of misappropriating about $1,100 from the First National Bank of Austin. He had been railroaded to prison. I believe it.

It was not his guilt that I thought of as he stood at my door that Sunday morning, but his buoyant friendship and the odd, delightful gravity of his quiet speech. He held me as he had the first day I met him in the Honduras cantina

But as he left, a thought full of a stinging irritation wedged itself into these happier memories. I had been in prison nearly four weeks. Bill Porter knew it. Every one in the penitentiary knew it. He had taken his time about visiting me. Had it been me, I would have rushed to see him at the first opportunity.

I tried to make out a brief for him. Porter was a valuable man in prison. He had been a pharmacist in Greensboro before entering the bank at Austin. This experience won him the envied position of drug clerk in the prison hospital. Many privileges softened the bitterness of convict life. He had a good bed, decent food and comparative freedom. Why had he failed to visit me?

He was busy, I know. And he would have gone to almost any extremity to avoid asking a favor from the guard. It would have cut him to the quick to win a refusal from these men who were his inferiors. Was he merely waiting his easy opportunity to see me?

I didn't understand Bill Porter then as I learned to know him later. I know now the reason for that long delay. I can appreciate the goading humiliation O. Henry suffered when he stood before my cell acknowledging himself a criminal even as myself. Porter knew my high esteem for him. Always reticent, it was an aching blow to his pride to meet me now, no longer the gentleman, but the fellow convict.

CHAPTER XV.

Despair; attempt at escape; in the hell-hole; torture in the prison; the
diamond-thief's revenge; the flogging; hard labor; a message
of hope from O. Henry.

Weeks went by. I didn't see Porter again. The promise of help and a position in the hospital, where food was good and beds clean, had put a flavor even into prison stew. I counted on Porter. Gradually the confidence waned. I grew bitter with resentment and a cold feeling of abandonment. I had been used ragged by every one. It began to eat in on me that Bill was one with all the other ingrates I had helped.

I did not know that he was working for me all the while. I did not realize the obstacles that block promotion in a prison. I decided to help myself. I tried to escape, was caught, sent into solitary for 14 days and then brought down from the hell-hole for trial.

Dick Price, a convict I had befriended and a life termer, tried to save me. While I was sitting on the bench outside the deputy warden's room, Dick went past me.

"You've got a fellow Jennings in solitary for trying to escape. I gave him the saws. He's a new man. Ain't been here long enough to know the ropes. I wised him up to escape. Give me the punishment."

Dick spoke in a loud voice. I knew it was a cue

for me.   He had not given me the saws.   He knew nothing about the escape until a horse-thief peached on me.

I was called before the deputy.

"How did you like your new home?" he asked with a leer.   He meant the "hole" in solitary.   "I found where you got the saws."

"Dick Price had nothing to do with it."

"I thought so," he said.   "Dick's a 'mighty good boy.   Been here a 'mighty long time.   Come clean on this now and I'll make it easy for you."

"I can't."

"You'll have to."

"I can't."

"By God, I'll make you."   I knew what he meant. It made me desperate with fury.

"By God, you won't."

"Here, take this fellow down and give him seventy-five."

Only a man who has been in hell's mouth—who has seen the blood spurt as men, stripped and chained, are beaten until their flesh is torn and broken as a derelict, knows the indignity and depravity of a prison beating.   I saw myself cowed by this screaming brutality.   It made a fiend of me.

"You take me, you damn' coward; you strip me and beat me over that trough—try it, and if I live through it, I'll come back and cut your damn' throat!"

The deputy reared from me, his face ashen with rage.   Like a tortured maniac, I sprang at him.   The guards rushed forward, made a leap at me, stopped abruptly, livid and simpering, as though suddenly stricken. If any one of them had touched me I could have torn him to pieces.

I was ready to be killed outright sooner than submit to the horrors of that "punishment cell." I had seen too much of it—the prison demon dragged out of solitary and whipped into bleeding insensibility a couple of times a week—other prisoners given the "water" until their faces were one red, gushing stream and the anguished screams filled the air.

The basement where these things were done was directly under the hospital. I passed above it and I could look down on the way to the transfer office. Three weeks before a man had been beaten to death over that trough. The awful debauchery of that murder had seared into my brain.

The man was a friend of mine and one of the most intelligent convicts in the prison. He was a diamond robber—the cleverest crook in the pen, a man of neat speech and cultured manner. He had stolen some of the most priceless gems in the State. All the detectives in the country had not been able to locate the jewels. The jewelers offered thousands in a reward for the recovering of the diamonds. No third degree, no punishment could force from the man the location of his treasure.

In the prison was an editor, sentenced for the murder of a rival newspaper publisher. This fellow would have crucified his own mother to gain an extra crust for himself. He was always worming his way into favor by snitching on convicts. For some strange reason—perhaps because of their intellectual equality, he and the diamond robber became friends.

One morning the newspapers carried blazing headlines. The stolen diamonds had been found. The robber's secret was out.

Suspense and a surcharged excitement held the prison in a grip. We knew the episode was not closed. We waited.

The diamond robber said nothing. Restless curiosity sent its questions and suppositions across the "grapevine route" from one cell block to another. "Who had told?" "What would happen?"

The answer came in a sudden viciousness that revealed the whole betrayal. The robber sneaked one day down the corridor. He had a bottle in his hand. He had calculated his time. He fell into line just as the editor was going to his cell.

There was a frenzied scream, a moment's scuffle, a loud, prolonged, tormented cry. * The editor lay on the corridor floor, one eye burned out and his face puffed and flaming with the carbolic acid that was eating into his flesh. When he came out from the hospital he was half blinded and his face, such a seamy mass of ugly scars, hell itself wouldn't own him. He had won the confidence of the diamond-thief and betrayed him.

"Seventy-five" was the punishment ordered for the robber for the assault on a fellow prisoner. He was a tall, slender fellow, graceful and muscular—made like a white marble statue.

Prison is not the place for dark dealings. Every convict knew in less than an hour that the robber was to "get his." I walked out from the transfer office and looked down the stairs into the basement. The robber, strapped across the trough, his ankles drawn under it, his arms across the top, was already a mass of blood.

He uttered not the slightest moan. None but a hell hound—and that's what a guard becomes when he has done a thing like this a hundred times—could have laid those heavy paddles, with their edges sharp as razor blades, across that raw and jagged flesh. The robber was beaten to the bone. Long after he was unconscious, the merciless flaying went on.

The guards stopped. Half an hour passed. The robber came to. The guards propped him up. The deputy warden glowered over him.

"Now say that you are sorry. Say that you'll obey the rules," he thundered.

The mangled, bleeding victim, who couldn't stand, couldn't speak, raised a gray, death-stricken face. And after a long pause, a husky curse came from his lips.

"—— —— him, I wish I got his other eye."

They strapped him back to the trough and hacked him to death. Broken bones, ragged flesh, they struck into it until it doubled a limp mass into the trough.

That's what "seventy-five" meant in the Ohio penitentiary in 1899.

They called me a man-killer. I never murdered a man in my life. I shot quick and clean in self-defense. I would have felt myself a degraded beast to have foully killed like that.

If that warden had carried out his sentence, he would have died like a cur. He knew it.

I was reduced to the fourth grade, given a suit of white with black stripes running horizontally across it, put in with the lockstep gang and sent to the bolt contract to work.

The confinement, the isolation, the cruel discipline took the spirit out of me. I heard from no one. No one was allowed to see me. Papers, books, visitors were denied me.

And then I faked sick just to get a word to Porter.

The "croaker" was taking my temperature. Bill came out of the prescription-room; he was not allowed to speak to me. His look was enough. Bitter, sad, troubled. He nodded to me and turned his back. I knew that Bill had tried and failed. He was powerless to help me.

I went back to the bolt works. This is the hardest labor in the prison. Outside contractors pay the State about 30 cents a day for the hire of the men. If a given task is not finished on time the convict is sent to the hole for punishment. Twice in three days "Little Jim," a negro, was given the "water."

A hose with a nozzle, one-quarter of an inch in diameter, sixty pounds pressure behind it, sends a stream of terrific force at the prisoner. His head is held strapped, the stream that is hard as steel is turned full in the man's face, his eyes, his nostrils. The pressure compels him to open his mouth. The swift, battering deluge tears down his throat and rips his stomach in two. No man can stand the "water" twice and live.

Little Jim passed my bench one morning.

"Mr. Al, they done give Lil Jim the water ag'in,"

he whispered, walked a step, flopped to the ground, a red geyser spouting from his mouth. Before Little Jim reached the hospital he was dead.

After that morning, I was about finished. I lost all hope, all ambition. Bill Porter saved me.

Across the grapevine route he sent his message. From one convict to another the word went until it was stealthily whispered in my ear:

"Don't lose heart. I'm working. There's a new main finger."

CHAPTER XVI

The new main finger; a tuba solo; failure at prayer; transfer to the post-office; literary ambition; O. Henry writes a story.

The new "main finger" meant a new warden and an entire change of administration. A shift like this sent the prison into feverish, suppressed excitement.

I was working at the bolt contract. A patrol guard glided to my bench in the shop and silently beckoned to me. There is something mischievously sinister in the hushed voices and the noiseless tread of men in prison. Without a word, without even knowing where I was going, I followed.

I was taken out of the fourth grade when I arrived at the State shop.

"Think you could play a tuba solo Sunday?" the guard asked. "You're going back to your place in the band."

Musicians are scarce enough in prison. I had been one of the dominant notes in the band before I was thrown into solitary.

Sunday the new warden was to publicly take office. Several hundred visitors would be present. The warden would make his speech to the 1,700 convicts. The prison band would furnish entertainment.

As I passed through the chaplain's office into the library, where the band met before going to the rostrum, Bill Porter stood at the door. Quite dignified as always, but his face set, almost despondent, Porter greeted me.

"Colonel, you are looking better. Thank God they needed the tuba solo." He lowered the tone that was always hesitant and whispering. "I think, pardner, you are in a religious fervor. There is a vacancy in the chaplain's office. Do you think you could pray?"

I don't know whether I was happier at the prospect of leaving the bolt shop or in the assurance that Porter had won me back in the band and was as loyal to me as I would have been to him.

"Pray! Hell, yes, Bill. Sure I can pray if it will get me off the contract."

How many prayers we offered just to get us "off the contract." Porter smiled.

"Never think that I forget you, colonel. Believe me, that my thoughts were with you every time a poor, outraged devil sent his screams up from the basement."

I looked at Porter, surprised at the tense emotion in his voice. His lips quivered and a sort of gray blight seemed spreading over his face.

"I can't drag out much longer," he said.

It was one of the few times that Porter ever voiced his loathing of the prison system of punishments, and yet he knew perhaps more of its ghastly outrages than any other convict.

Porter had already been night clerk at the hospital for a year and a half. He saw the broken bodies brought up from the basement when men were all but done to death in vicious floggings, in the water and in the hangings. He saw the doctors work over these tortured wrecks, and heal them just so that they could be further tormented.

And when some bitter wretch, driven desperate and insane, would attempt suicide in his cell, Porter was always forced to accompany the prison doctor and aid him to revive the convict. These attempted suicides were almost a nightly occurrence. Often they succeeded.

Comparatively easy as a place in the hospital was, no toil could have corroded into the heart of a man of Porter's temperament as did this unabating contact with misery.

He used to come into the post-office and sit for hours, dumb with a bleak, aching despair. In the blithest moments of his success in New York, Porter could never shake himself free from the clawing shadow of the prison walls.

Porter got me into the chaplain's office, but I didn't make good. I couldn't see my way clear to join the Sunday school. The chaplain took a violent grudge against me the day after my arrival. It was noon on a Wednesday when the minister and two convicts passed through the outer office into the chaplain's private study. One of the converts was a regular spittoon bully, in for horse-stealing; the other was a cheap vaudeville actor. He had cut his wife's throat. They were not in my class.

"We're going to pray," the chaplain informed me.

"That's all right with me," I answered.

He scowled at me, his face white with irritation,

his puny voice shrilling out, "Aren't you going in to pray?"

"No. Not with that crowd."

The nigger horse-thief, the cut-throat and the minister went into the study and the chaplain stood while the convicts threw themselves on their knees and immediately began mumbling and moaning to the Creator.

An hour later I was sent to the deputy warden for insolence and insubordination. He dismissed the charge.

"You don't have to pray if you don't want to. That ain't what you're sent to the pen for."

I was given a job in the post-office. Billy Raidler, another train-robber, was chief post-office clerk. In this new position I had considerable liberty, I was near to the hospital. Bill Porter, Raidler and I cemented a friendship that lasted until the death, first of Porter, then of Raidler.

Raidler was the most beloved man in the pen. He had been the terror of the Indian Territory in his outlaw days. Yet he was slender, fair-haired, soft-voiced as a girl. He had an impish wit and the most obliging nature of any man I ever met. In his last fight with the marshals he had lost three fingers of his right hand. Two bullets caught him in the neck, knocking his spine askew. He walked as though he had locomotor ataxia.

Bill Porter was just as much the recluse in prison as he had been in Honduras and Mexico. He did not make friends readily. Between him and the world was an impassable barrier. No man was privileged to break down that wall which hid his hopes, his thoughts, his troubles. And so he liked the outlaw prisoners better than other men. They had learned the fine art of indifference to the other fellow's affairs.

In the post-office, Billy Raidler, Porter and I passed many a happy hour. I came to see a new Porter, who afterward developed into O. Henry, the smile-maker.

The discovery came about in a peculiar manner.

I had started to write the memoirs of my bandit days. Every man in prison is writing a story. Each man considers his life a tragedy—an adventure of the most absorbing interest. I had given my book a fine title. Raidler was enthusiastic about it. He gloried in "my flow of language."

"The Long Riders" was galloping ahead at a furious stride. There were chapters in it with 40,000 words and not one climax. There were other chapters with but seven sentences and as many killings as there were words.

Raidler insisted that a man be shot in every paragraph. It would make the book "go," he said. Finally I came to a halt.

"If I have any more men killed," I said, "there'll be nobody left on earth."

"I'll tell you what you do," Raidler said. "You ask Bill Porter about it. He's writing a story, too."

At that moment I felt myself far the greater writer of the two. I had not even known that Porter hoped to write. He dropped in to see us in the afternoon.

"Bill tells me you're writing a story," I said. Porter looked at me quickly, a dark flush staining his cheek.

"No, I'm not writing, I'm just practicing," he said.

"Oh, is that all?" I felt really sorry for the man who was destined to write the finest stories America ever read.

"Well, I'm writing one. In fact, it's almost finished. Come in and I'll read it to you."

Porter left the room quickly. I never saw him for two weeks.

A desk and a chair inside the railing of the prison drug store—the five wards of the hospital grouped around that store and in those wards from 50 to 200 patients racked with all manner of disease. The quiet of the night disturbed with the groans of broken men, the coughs of the wasted, the frightened gasp of the dying. The night nurse padding from ward to ward and every once in a while returning to the drug store with the crude information—another "con" has croaked. Then, down the corridors the rattle of the wheelbarrow and the negro life termer bumping the "stiff" to the dead house. A desk and a chair settled in the raw heart of chill depression!

There at that desk, night after night, sat Bill Porter. And in the grisly atmosphere of prison death and prison brutality there bubbled up the mellow smile of his genius—the smile born of heartache, of shame, of humiliation—the smile that has sent its ripple of faith and understanding to the hearts of men and women everywhere.

When it first caught Billy Raidler and me, we

cried outright. I think it was about the proudest moment in O. Henry's life. He had come into the prison post-office on a Friday afternoon. It was just about a fortnight after I had offered to read him my memoirs.

"Colonel, would you mind granting me an audience," he said in the bantering formality of his way. "I'd appreciate the opinion of a fellow-struggler. I have a little scrap here. I'd like to read it to you and Billy."

Porter was usually so reticent, usually the listener while others talked, that one felt a warm surge of pleasure whenever he showed a disposition for confidence. Billy and I swerved about, eager for the reading.

Porter sat on a high stool near the desk and carefully drew from his pocket a roll of brown paper. He had written in a big, generous hand and there was scarcely a scratch or an erasure on a single sheet.

From the moment that Porter's rich, low, hesitant voice began there was a breathless suspense until suddenly Billy Raidler gulped, and Porter looked up as one aroused from a dream. Raidler grinned and jabbed his maimed hand into his eye.

"Damn you, Porter, I never did it in my life before. By God, I didn't know what a tear looked like."

It was a funny thing to see two train-robbers blubbering over the simple story.

Perhaps the convict is over-sentimental, but the queer twist in Porter's story just seemed to sneak into the heart with a kind of overflowing warmth.

It was "The Christmas Chaparral" he read to us. Both Billy and I could understand the feelings of the cowpuncher who had lost out in the wooing of the girl. We could feel his hot jealousy toward the peeler who won the bride. We knew that he would keep his promise—we knew he would return to kill his rival.

And when he comes back on Christmas Eve, dressed as a Santa Claus, armed to bring tragedy to the happy ranch house, we could sympathize with his mood. He overhears the wife say a word in his defense—he hears her praise the early kindness of his life. He walks up to her—"There's a Christmas present in the next room for you," he says, and leaves the house without firing the shot that was to have ended the husband's life.

Well, the story is told as only O. Henry can rough in the picture. Billy and I could see ourselves in the cowpuncher's place. We could feel ourselves respond to that stray beam of kindness in the girl's thoughtless praise. We could feel it and it brought the tears to our calloused old cheeks.

Porter sat there silent, pleased, his eyes aglow with happy satisfaction. He rolled up the manuscript and climbed down from the stool.

"Gentlemen, many thanks. I never expected to win tears from experts of your profession," he said at last. And then we all fell into a speculation as to what the story should bring and where we ought to send it. We felt an interest in its fate. "The Long Riders" and its many buckets of blood were forgotten in the wizardry of "The Christmas Chaparral."

With the fervor of hero-worshipers, Raidler and I acknowledged Bill Porter, the genius.

We decided to send the story to the *Black Cat*. There was in the prison at this time a cultured Frenchman, a banker from New Orleans. Through his sister, Porter's stories, bearing the New Orleans address, were sent to the editor.

When "The Christmas Chaparral" was sent out, Billy and I could hardly wait for the weeks to go by. We were sure it would be accepted at once. At least $75 was the price we thought it ought to bring. It came back.

Years later I peddled my own story from editor to editor. Never did I feel the angry spasm of disappointment that seized me when Porter's great story was rejected.

I knew that he, too, was filled with a bitter regret. He had counted on the money. He wanted to send a little present to his daughter, Margaret. Now she would have to wait. It cut him to the quick, this failure of his, as a father.

But he said very little when Billy handed him the package. We were so incensed against the publishers, of the magazines, we wanted him to blacklist them in the future.

"Colonel, the day may come when I can decline publication—at present I don't seem to have the deciding voice."

And he went back to his desk and wrote and wrote. He went back to the melancholy prison hospital, to the night patrol through the cell ranges, gathering his material, transmuting the gloom through the

O. Henry alchemy into the sunny gold of his stories. Many of these he read to us in the stolen happiness of Sunday afternoons at the "Recluse Club."

CHAPTER XVII.

O. Henry, bohemian; the Recluse Club in the prison; the vanishing kitchen; the tragedy of Big Joe; effect on O. Henry; personality of a genius.

Porter was a bohemian in heart, in soul, in temperament. Not the poser—he had neither sympathy nor kinship with the temperamental quacks of the artistic world—but a born original. He loved freedom and unconventional sociability. In this buoyant atmosphere he could warm up, whisper out his drolleries, forget. Even in the prison the whimsical vagabond in him asserted itself. He founded the "Recluse Club."

Six convicts, three of them bank-robbers, one a forger and two train-robbers, made up its membership. We met on Sunday in the construction office. And never a club in the highest strata of society had graver, brighter, happier discussion—never an epicure's retreat served a more delicious ménu than our Sunday repasts.

The embezzlers had been men of great wealth. They were educated and polished. It was a fitting environment to bring out the best in Bill Porter. He was king of that exclusive club.

It was a Sunday, three weeks after I had been transferred to the post-office, that I was invited to join.

"Slither over, colonel," Porter whispered to me. "Ikey will show you the way."

An odder initiation ceremony never was held.

Porter met me at the door of the construction office and with elaborate burlesque paid tribute to my accomplishments. "Here is a financier worthy to sit with the elect. The colonel kills with a deft equanimity equaled only by the finesse of Louisa in seasoning the gravy."

Louisa was the nickname given to the French gentleman sent to the Ohio penitentiary on a charge of embezzlement. He was dapper, swarthy, mannered like a prince—the chief clerk in the construction office and the man responsible for the magic kitchenette concealed behind the walls of the office.

Louisa was official chef of the "Recluse Club." He turned out mince pies and roast beef that would have made the eyes of Dives bulge with envy. He measured to the grain all his ingredients and he followed minutely the instructions in a big cook book.

If the prison had suddenly been changed into paradise it would have seemed no more miraculous than the scene in this improvised banquet room. A fairy table, decorated with wild flowers and set for six, was laden with all manner of delicacies—olives, radishes, sugar, cream, white bread, lettuce, tomatoes.

In an armchair sat the little, rotund banker from New Orleans—the one who had accosted me the day I transferred myself to the cell in Bankers' Row. He was such a sputtery, rasp-voiced, punctilious trifle, Porter could not abide him. Billy Raidler was also sitting in comfortable grandeur. These two were exempt from labor—Billy because he could not walk alone; Carnot because he was old and fussy as a fat, spoiled baby.

Ikey slippered from wall to wall, his ear tuned for the sound of the guard's approach. The club and its opulent layout was distinctly against prison rules. At a moment's signal, gas stove and its range could be hidden out of sight. Louisa was an architect and draughtsman.

A false wall had been built and the kitchenette with full equipment was hidden like a long telephone booth behind it. It was stocked with silverware, napkins, flavoring extracts, flour and every necessity, enough in fact, for a small hotel. All had been stolen or bargained from the head clerks in other shops and from the chief cook in the kitchen.

Louisa dodged from behind the door, a great dish cloth tied about his waist.

"Dinner is served, gentlemen. Make yourselves at home."

It was Bill Porter's turn to wait on table. Bill in all his buoyant sunniness brought on the roast beef that gala Sunday. It seemed to give him a whimsical satisfaction to wait on Raidler and me.

"Colonel, I feel more at home holding the tray for you than I would have felt holding the horses that day," he whispered in my ear.

Louisa, the chef, carved. I'll remember to my last breath the ménu. It was the first good meal I had had since I was thrown into jail to await trial three years before.

We had a tomato soup that was the pride of

Louisa's art. He boasted of the pinch of soda added to keep the milk from curdling. And there was corn and green peas and roast potatoes, a mince pie and a cold bread pudding made with raisins and currants.

I've given that recipe of Louisa's to every woman I ever met. Not one of them could turn out the delicacy as the chef of the "Recluse Club" did it.

Porter had drafted the rules of the club. A copy lay at each place with the little cartoons he made of us. Funny little verses were scrawled under the figures. Every Sunday we had different place cards.

Porter's raillery was boundless. Raidler and I were the only ones to acknowledge ourselves guilty. Louisa, Porter, Ikey and old Carnot were all victims of circumstances. They were touchy about their pasts. And so the cartoonist drew them as cherubs, friars, lilies without stain and the dewdrops glistening on their white sheafs.

Not one of those men, and they were Porter's equals at least in social position, dared to take liberties with him. I think they held him in a sort of awe. His dignity was invulnerable. Old Carnot would have liked the same respect. He never got it. Billy Raidler never tired of puncturing his pompous self-esteem. But Billy would have died rather than wound Bill Porter.

Old Carnot did not want any one even to mention the fact that he was in the penitentiary. He would bluster and sputter when any one spoke of him as a convict. Every Sunday there was an argument about it. Raidler, just for the impish love of teasing the old man, would open it.

"Now, Mr. Carnot," he would say, "my esteemed friend, Bill Porter, and I propose to found a union of ex-convicts as soon as we are discharged. We wish you to join."

Carnot would get red, champ his teeth together and rustle in his chair.

"Don't speak of it. I don't wish you to mention it." His pursy lips sent out a shower, I ducked.

"Colonel, I don't know why you are contorting your face and capering about so," the old man turned on me.

"Well, by God, your honor, I don't want to get drowned."

Then it would begin all over again, Carnot protesting that any man who would salute him as an ex-convict would be shot on the spot. No man dreaded the thought of that stigma more than Porter. We had many talks about it. He hid his feeling under a light banter.

Once in a while the veneer cracked. The day I told him about the ugly tragedy of Big Joe, a Creek Indian of the "Buck Gang," I thought he was going to faint. His face was usually quiet and enigmatic in its expression. This day it got ashen and rigid. He said nothing for a moment. Then with a flash he turned the subject. Old Carnot would not have it. There was almost an open breach between them.

Big Joe had been sick at the hospital for months. One night the word went around that he had croaked. A burglar friend of mine, on patrol duty at the hospital, came over to the post-office.

"Jennings, come along over to the ward with me.

I want to show you something," he said mysteriously.

"What's up?"

"They've got Big Joe tied up ready for the wheel-barrow and he isn't dead."

"Hell, no!"

"Come over and see."

I went in with him. Big Joe was lying in his cot, his feet tied together, a handkerchief over his eyes.

"Look, the burglar whispered. He took out his penknife and pricked the Indian on the foot. The knee drew up, the man twitched to his neck. It made me sick with repulsion. I went over to Porter.

"Big Joe isn't dead," I said. "Tell the croaker."

"The damn' hellions know it," Porter hissed. "I told him. They'd like to bury us all alive. Damn them, I'll get them yet."

He turned his back and rushed off. I went back to the cot where the Indian's body lay.

Porter came back with the night doctor. Big Joe had already opened his eyes. As the croaker took up his wrist to feel his pulse he yanked himself suddenly to one side.

"Drink—water!" The broken mumble seemed to splinter the air. The four of us stepped back with the shock of this whisper from the lips of the man tied up as dead.

The doctor himself pulled off the straps. The burglar ran for the water. I went back to the post-office.

The next night Big Joe had another fit.

"He's dead this time." The croaker was still shaky from his recent experience. "Let him stay dead. I don't want any of you damn' meddlers to monkey with him."

The gigantic body, yellow and emaciated, was carted to the dead house and laid in the bottom of the trough. This trough stood on the cement floor and was about three feet deep. The stiff was placed on it and cracked ice scattered over it. The body was kept a day. If no friends called for it the doctors held a dissecting symposium—what was left of the bones was dumped into a rough board box and stuck into a hole in the prison graveyard.

It was a Saturday night when Big Joe kicked off. The night porter used to go whistling by the post-office, jogging the wheelbarrow to the dead house. He would stop for a word with Billy and me. We would look out. Sometimes there would be one stiff with its arms and legs dangling over the sides of the cart. Sometimes there were two or even three.

"Big Joe done got it foh shuah dis time," he sang out to us, and clattered blithely on.

There was something callous and appalling about the prison attitude to the stiffs. The men were treated as so much refuse—they got no more respect than a dead dog. Big Joe's "comeback" had given me an odd twist. I felt spooky, bitter, depressed.

I went over to the dead house on Sunday morning. Curiosity drew me. It was just a dark shack, 'way off near the gas house. The patrol guard went with me. We pushed the door to.

The horror of the thing struck upon us. It was revolting as though a cold clammy hand reached up from that trough and smeared us with blood. A kind of strangling sensation caught me. The guard hung to my waist, his teeth chattering. Big Joe had been placed in the bottom of the trough. He had "come to" again.

He had awakened in the dead house in the middle of the night. He had tried to climb out. His clawing, terrible, long arms were flung forward. His body hung over the board, his head resting on the cement, as though he had lost his balance and half toppled out. The face, one cheek pressed against the ground, was twisted toward us—the mouth agape, the eyes staring.

I went over to the club shortly after 12. Louisa and Porter were in the little box kitchen. Louisa had his dishrag apron tied about him. Porter, immaculate in the prison gray, was wearing a rich blue necktie.

The clerk in the State shop used to make us presents in return for favors. We wore the finest grade of underwear; we had good white shirts. Except for the black stripe on the trousers we could look like "dandies" on occasions. It was always an occasion for Porter. Even in his blackest moods—and he had many of them in prison—he was fastidious about his appearance.

Louisa and Porter were scrapping like a couple of old women over the roast. Porter was a bit of an epicure, and there was many a heated argument over culinary niceties.

"Here, taste it, then," the chef jabbed the spoon between Porter's teeth.

"A little more celery salt," Porter smacked his tongue against the roof of his mouth, paused a moment after the manner of the queen's taster, and gave his opinion.

"Now here, I measured it three times." Louisa produced the cook book to prove it.

"That is no proof. You should have an apothecary's scale and weigh the ingredients," Porter was in one of his bubbling, irrepressible moods. "Let the colonel judge between us." He turned to me, and stopped, with the spoon clanking to the floor. "By God, Al, what ails you?"

I said nothing for a moment. We were seated about the table. They pressed me. I told them about Big Joe. I couldn't seem to keep it to myself. Porter jumped up and slammed his chair against the wall. Old Carnot commenced to sputter.

"We should write to the President of the United States about it." Carnot would never stoop to any lesser authority. "It is an outrage."

Porter came back to the table, the explosive, unusual outburst over. He drew in his lip and coughed —a habit of his.

"I think the summer will be quite warm," he offered.

Carnot would not have it.

"Mr. Porter, you should exercise your best ability as a writer on this subject. You should enkindle the world about it. You should put it in an article and send it broadcast."

Porter's cold look would have chilled the ardor of any other suggestion-giver.

"I do not understand you, sir," he answered frigidly. "I am not here as a reporter. I shall not take upon myself the burden of responsibility. This prison and its shame is nothing to me."

He got up and walked into the kitchen. I followed him. "There are some obnoxious people here." His voice was stifled with resentment. "We should eliminate them."

It was one of the few times that I ever saw Bill Porter openly ruffled. He despised tips from men of Carnot's caliber. He never wanted any one to point out a story to him. He had to see the thing himself. As he says in "The Duplicity of Hargreaves"—"All life belongs to me. I take thereof what I want. I return it as I can."

With Billy Raidler and me it was quite different. Porter liked us. He would sit in the post-office and deliberately draw out from us accounts of the outlaw days. He would get us to describe the train-robbers, he would deftly prod us into giving elaborate details even to the very slang expressions the men had used in their talk. I never saw him take a note, but his memory was relentless.

The day I told him about Dick Price, a fellow-convict, he sat quiet for a long time.

"That will make a wonderful story," he said at last.

Dick Price is the original of the immortal Jimmy Valentine.

Porter came into the post-office just after the astounding feat had been accomplished. Dick Price, the warden, and I had returned from the offices of the Press-Post Publishing Company. Price had opened the safe in 10 seconds.

CHAPTER XVIII.

Story of convict Dick Price; grief for his mother; her visit to the prison; the safe-opening; promise of pardon.

Porter gives Dick the chance in the story that he never had in life. The history of the real Jimmy Valentine, shadowed, embittered, done to death in the stir, was just another of the tragedies that ripped through the film and showed Bill Porter the raw, cruel soul of the "upper crust."

Dick Price had been in prison ever since he was a little fellow of 11. There were a few wretched years in the outer world. It was not freedom.

Bill Porter took but one incident out of that tragic life for his story, "A Retrieved Reformation." His Jimmy Valentine is a rather debonair crook—but in the moment when he throws off his coat, picks up his tools and starts to open the safe, in that moment there is crowded the struggle and the sacrifice of a lifetime. It goes to the heart, quick and piercing, when Jimmy's chance of happiness seems lost; it sends the breath into the throat with a quiver of joy when he wins out in the end. Porter has touched the strings so deftly because the whole shadow of Dick Price's broken life hovers in the background of the story.

Dick was what convicts call a "stir bug." He had been in the pen so long he had become morose, sour, a brooding sort. But he was as square a man as Christ

ever put on the earth. Dick was the fellow that tried
to save me from the beating and the contract after my
attempt to escape. I had done him a little favor and
he was ready to have his flesh torn to ribbons in gratitude.

He was in under the "habitual criminal act." In
Ohio a man caught at his third offense is given a life
sentence in the penitentiary and denied all privileges.
Only the man that has been half blinded in solitary,
that has been cooped in wretched cells and denied the
right to read or write—only the fellow that has had
the spirit beaten down in him by the agonized screams
of tortured men, can know what Dick Price's sentence meant.

He was about 20 when he was thrown into prison
on his third offense. And because it was the third he
was robbed of all human comforts. He couldn't have
a book or a paper. He wasn't allowed to write a letter; he wasn't even allowed to receive one. And if
there was a kind, anxious soul in the outer world
eager to hear from him, to see him, it made no difference. For 16 years not one stray word, not one bit
of cheer had come to him from the world.

I never saw anything so terrible as the way that
fellow's heart was breaking. He had an eternal hankering to hear from his old mother. It whipped him
ceaselessly. He wanted to know if she was alive, if
she had to work as hard as before, if she thought of
him. He had a passion to get a word from her that
was driving him mad.

I got the word for him. And he was ready to die
for me in his gratitude. Because of that word he

opened the safe of the Press-Post Publishing Company.

I met Dick first walking about the cell ranges at night. It was just a few months after I arrived. I was in the transfer office and was about the last man to be locked up. Dick had been there so long the deputies trusted him and gave him passes to leave his cell and wander about the corridors. I used to see his small, nervous figure pacing back and forth. He had a keen, dark face and a restless gray eye. One night I came upon him sitting in a corner, eating a piece of pie.

"Have a slice, pardner?" he called to me. The other men shunned Dick a bit because he was moody and nerve-racked—because, too, he had a sharp, almost brilliant mind, much superior to the average convict.

I accepted, and it was then that he told me of his longing for news of his mother. "I tell you it's hell, to think the way she's made to suffer. I'll bet you she stands outside these infernal walls at night—I'll bet she'd tear her heart out to hear from me. You know—"

Dick swung into his story. Men in prison hunger for conversation. They will tell their histories to any one who will listen to them.

Little Dick was a gutter snipe, he said. His father was a Union soldier He died of delirium tremens when Dick was a few years old. After that the kid just belonged down in the alley with the tin cans. His mother took in washing. She tried to give the boy enough to eat. She sent him to school. Sometimes there was soup and bread for dinner; sometimes Dick took his meals out of the rubbish piles.

And one day the poor, ravenous little ragpicker broke into a box car and stole a 10-cent box of crackers.

"And they sent me to hell for the rest of my life for that," a look of bitterness lashed like a dark wave over his face. "I might have put these to good use if I'd had a chance." He looked down at his hands. They were the strongest, most perfectly shaped hands I have ever seen. The fingers were long and tapered, muscular yet delicate. "They said my mother didn't take care of me. They sent me to the Mansfield reformatory and they turned me out a master mechanic at 18."

His graduation papers were of no value. A man named E. B. Lahman controlled all the bolt works in the Ohio penitentiary. Convicts loathed him, and because he knew the danger of employing any upon their discharge, he made it a rule that no ex-convict would be given work in his shops. Dick Price had a job there. Somebody found that he had been dragged up in a reform school. He was fired.

He couldn't get a job. His mechanical training made him adept at safe-manipulating. He cracked one, took a few hundred dollars, got a jolt for it.

It was the same story again when he was released. No one would give him a job. He could starve or steal. He cracked another safe, got caught and was given life.

"You know, the old woman came to the court," he told me. "And, gee, I can hear it yet, the way she bawled when they took me away. It's just awful. You know, Jennings, if you could write to her, I'd die for you."

I managed to get a note smuggled out to her. The most pitiful broken, little mispelled scrawl I ever saw came back.

And when that bent, heart-broken old mother stumbled across the guardroom floor and stood with her feeble hands shaking the wicket, I'd like to have died. I couldn't speak. Neither could she.

She just stood there with the tears running down her rough cheeks and her poor chin trembling.

Dick's mother had a faded red shawl wrapped about her head. She was twisted and bent. A bit of gray hair, coarse and curly, fell over her ear. She had fixed herself up, thinking she might catch a glimpse of her boy.

"And they won't let his old mother see the lad, my poor little Dick—the poor child!" The sobs caught in her throat. She pressed her face against the wicket, her gnarled wasted hands shaking the iron bars.

The poor old creature was just crazy for a sight of her son. Dick was not 100 yards away. They wouldn't let these two have that scrap of joy. Not in four million years could the law understand the agony it had wrought.

"But I thought I might catch the look of him, by chance, maybe." She looked up at me with a pitiful hope in her dim eyes. It hurt the heart to wound the poor creature. I had to tell her that Dick could not come, that I had sent for her, that I would tell

Dick anything she wanted to say, that she must not let the guards know who she was.

"Dick is the foreman of the machine shop and the smartest man in the prison," I told her. A prideful smile came like a sunbeam into her eye.

"Sure, I know it, that pert he was a baby." She began to grope into the pocket of her skirt and brought out an envelope tied in red ribbon. Carefully wrapped in brown paper were a couple of pictures. One was of a big-eyed, laughing youngster of four or five.

"A prettier bairn never drew breath. 'Tis happy we were in that time. 'Twas before the drink got the better of poor John."

The other picture was of Dick just before he had been arrested the last time. He was a boy of 19. The face was sensitive, clean-looking, determined.

"He doesn't look chipper like that now," she looked at me hoping I would contradict her fears. "'Twas the gay tongue that he had and the laugh always in his heart. Such a tale as he would be telling me of the good home he would buy. The poor child, does it go very hard on him in here, he was that fond of a cheery place?"

Fifty questions she asked me. Every answer was a lie. The truth would have killed her as it was ending Dick.

I told her Dick was happy. I told her he was well. I said he might get a pardon. It was all I could do to talk. I knew that Dick was doomed. He was actually wasted with tuberculosis. But the promises seemed to give her comfort. She stood silent a moment.

"Will you be after telling him his old mother's prayers are with him? And just let on to him that I come down by the walls every blessed night to be that near to him."

Poor Dick, he was waiting in the range for me that night. He never said a word. He just looked at me. I told him everything she had said. I told him how pretty, like a grandmother, she looked. I said that she came down to the prison at night to pray for him. He didn't speak. He walked off. Four times he came back and tried to thank me. At last he sat down, covered his face with his hands and burst out crying.

It was only a few months later that I was caught trying to escape. Dick Price tried to take the punishment in my stead. He went to the deputy and swore he had given me the saws. It was a guard who had done it. If I had snitched on him he would have got ten years.

The deputy knew that Dick had lied. I told him that he did it in gratitude—that I had got a letter to his mother and he wanted to save me from the contract.

So I cleared him of the charge, but he was reduced to the fourth grade and compelled to fall in with the lockstep. It was going pretty hard with him. His work in the shop was exacting. Sometimes he would get a fit of coughing that left him weak for an hour.

When I was transferred to the post-office, I used

to go over and visit Dick. I had money then, too, and we used to swap pies and doughnuts. Dick would talk about the reform school. The things he told were appalling. They made me bitter with hatred. Little fellows of 11 or 12 were just put through a training school for hell.

Several times I tried to get another letter to the old woman. Something always happened.

After I had been appointed private secretary to the warden, it looked as though Dick's chance had come. He performed a service of great value to the State. He saved the papers of the Press-Post Publishing Company. The Governor promised him a pardon.

The Press-Post Publishing Company had been placed in the hands of a receiver. Wholesale charges of thievery were bandied about. The stockholders had been robbed. They blamed the directors, the directors put it up to the treasurer. They secured a warrant for his arrest. He locked the safe and fled.

Columbus was agog over the scandal. Some of the biggest men in the city were implicated. The court had to get the papers out of the safe. It occurred to somebody in authority that there might be a cracksman in the pen who could help them out of the difficulty. The warden was very eager to accommodate them.

"Is there any fellow here who can do it?" he asked me. Warden Darby was a prince. He had improved prison conditions. The men all liked him.

"There are perhaps forty here who can do it. I

can do it myself. A little nitroglycerine turns **any** combination."

"They can't take the risk of dynamite. They want the papers recovered intact."

I thought of Dick Price. He had told me of the method of safe-cracking which he had originated. He could open any combination on earth in from ten to fifteen seconds with his bare hands. A dozen times he had told me of the feat.

"See, I filed my nails to the quick," he said, "crosswise through the middle, until I filed them down to the nerve. It made them sensitive. I could feel the slightest jar. I held those fingers over the dial. I turned the combination with my right hand. The quiver of the tumbler passing its mark strikes through the nerves. I would stop, turn backward. It never failed."

I wondered if Dick would do the trick now for the State. "Could you get a pardon for him?" I asked the warden. Dick was really dying with his cough.

"If he'll do it, I'll move heaven and earth to win it."

I went to Dick. I told him he might get a pardon. His thin face flushed.

"She'd be glad. Hell, Al, I'd do anything for you."

The warden got a closed carriage. Early that afternoon the three of us went to the office of the Press-Post Publishing Company. Dick wanted me with him.

We scarcely spoke. There was a strained, nervous

hush over us. The warden fidgeted, lit a cigar, and let it go out without taking a puff. He was worried. So was I. I was afraid Dick couldn't make good. I figured that he probably had lost his art through disuse. Then it occurred to me that he might have exaggerated. Sixteen years in prison knocks the props from a man's brain often enough.

The warden had wired Governor George K. Nash of Ohio. He promised the pardon if the safe was opened. What a sore humiliation to Warden Darby if Dick failed!

Not a word had been said, but Dick looked up with that young, magnetic smile of his. "Don't Worry, Al," he grinned. "I'll rip hell out of it if it's made of cast iron and cement." His confidence made us feel easier.

"Give me the file." Dick had cautioned me to get him a small, rat-tailed file and to make sure that the edges were keen. I handed it to him. He scrutinized it as though he were a diamond-buyer looking for a yellow speck in a gem. Then he started to work. The warden and I shuddered.

Half way down the nail across the middle he drew the file. His nails were deep and beautifully shaped. Back and forth he filed until the lower half of the nail was separated from the upper by a thin red mark. He filed to the quick. Soon only the lower half of the nail remained.

Light and deft, his sensitive hand worked. I watched his face. It didn't even twitch. He was completely absorbed in the process and seemed to have forgotten the warden and me. Once or twice

he champed his teeth and his breath came a bit short.
The fingers bled a little. He took out his handkerchief and dabbed them clean. Then he sat back. He
was finished.

I took his hand and looked at it. It was a neat
job, but cruel. The index, middle and third fingers
of his left hand looked as though the nails had been
pared half off and the quick bruised and sandpapered.

Dick was so tense with suppressed excitement that
he bolted out of the carriage as soon as it stopped
and walked so quickly the warden and I had to run
to keep pace with him. When we reached the office
about a dozen men were waiting.

"Is this a show, Al?" Dick snapped the words
out. He was full of impatience. We stood around
about ten minutes. Dick looked at me angrily. I
was beset with alarm anyway. I took his look to
mean that his fingers wouldn't respond if we didn't
hurry. I ran over to the warden, bumping against
two gossipy, stupid looking officials.

"Hurry up or the job is up." His face took on
the scaredest, grayest shadow I ever saw. Dick put
his hand to his mouth and laughed. I whispered to
the warden that the men would have to remain outside. Only two State representatives, the warden,
Dick and I went into the room where the safe was
kept.

"That's it," one of the men said.

Dick went over to it. There wasn't a breath of
hesitation in his answer.

"Take the time, Al." There was a chuckle of

triumph in the challenge. His thin face was quiet as a statue's. The cheekbones were smudged with red and his eyes unnaturally brilliant.

He kneeled before the safe, put his bruised fingers across the dial, waited a moment, and then turned the combination. I watched every quiver of his strong, delicate hands. There was the slightest pause, his right hand went backward. He turned the dial again, pulled the knob gently toward him. The safe was opened!

The miracle seemed to strike everyone dumb. The room was stiller than silence. It was spellbound. The State officials stood as though riven. I looked at my watch. It was just twelve seconds since Dick had begun.

He got up and walked off. The warden sprang toward him. The tears were crowding into Darby's eyes. His face was flushed with pride. He put his arm on Dick's shoulder.

"That was fine, lad. God bless you!"

Dick nodded. He was an indifferent sort.

On the ride back to the pen the warden leaned over and put his hand on Dick's. "You're the noblest fellow God ever made," he said. "If they gave me the deal you got, hell itself wouldn't have made me do it."

Dick shrugged his shoulders and started to speak. His lip trembled. He looked out of the carriage window, watching the people and the houses. He couldn't keep his glance from the streets. He was leaning forward as though fascinated.

"Look at that, look at that!" He caught me

quickly and pointed to a little boy of ten or so carrying a rollicking youngster of three or four. I saw nothing unusual in the spectacle. Dick sank back as though a vision had passed.

"That's the first kid I've seen in sixteen years." He didn't look out again. We said nothing further during the drive back to the prison.

The next morning every newspaper in Columbus was full of the sensational story. The warden had given his word to Dick that the process would not be revealed. Not even the two men who had watched knew how the feat was accomplished. To them it seemed as witchcraft. All sorts of explanations were given.

A prisoner in the Ohio Penitentiary, serving a life term—a prisoner who had been sent up as a boy and who was now dying had opened the safe, with a steel wire, one daily said. Another paper said he used a paper-cutter. They were all mystified. Only one spoke of the pardon promised the convict. I went to the warden about it.

"Dick's cough is pretty bad. They ought to hurry it up."

"They will hurry," Darby promised. I know he meant what he said. I brought the word to Dick. He was back at the machine shop.

"I don't care," he said, in a fit of morose indifference. "I don't believe them. I did it for you, Al." He looked up quickly. "I wonder if the old woman saw the paper. I'd like her to know I did it. It would give her a sniff over the neighbors. Could you get her to know?" He walked to his cell and turned.

"Al," he said, "don't worry about me. I know I'll never get the pardon. I'm about done in, anyhow."

CHAPTER XIX

Interest of O. Henry; Price the original of Jimmy Valentine; the pardon denied; death of the cracksman; the mother at the prison gate.

When the cell door closed on Dick I stood watching the range, hoping he would come out again. In prison men grow superstitious. I wondered if his bitter conviction that the pardon would never be granted was a premonition. I went back to the office—the chill breath of fear putting down the ardent hope the warden's promise had raised.

Every man in the pen knew what Dick had done. They talked about it, advancing the most fantastic theories as to Dick's method.

Bill Porter came over to the warden's office that night. His visits were always welcome. There was in Bill's warm, quiet humor, a sunny cheer, an uplifting happiness that seemed to catch one by the neck of the spirit and shake him free from the harassing pettiness of prison life.

When Billy Raidler and I could not rouse each other, we kept our ears tuned for Bill's voice at the door. He would come in, sniff the moodiness in the air and breeze it away with a dash of his buoyant gaiety.

Bill's humor was not the offspark of happiness, but of the truth as he saw it. He was not an incorrigible optimist. There were times when silent gloom hovered like a black wraith about him. But he had an abiding faith in the worth of life and a sane, poised viewpoint that all the cruel injustice of his prison sentence could not distort.

Bill accepted life on its own terms. There was in him none of the futile cowardice that quarrels with the bargain of existence; mocks and sneers and exhausts itself in self-pity. To him life was but a colossal experiment marked by millions of inevitable failures, but destined, none the less, for an ultimate triumph.

His heart was crushed in prison, but his mind did not lose its clear, unbiased insight. He would send out a word, a phrase that seemed to puncture through the film of our dissatisfaction. The grotesque world, fabricated of depression, set itself aright and we were compelled to laugh and agree with Bill's droll honesty.

"Colonel, I surmise you were Pandora's imp when the Post's box of troubles was opened?" He handed me an account he had just read in one of the evening papers. It was the first time I had ever seen him manifest the slightest curiosity.

I told him about Dick. He wanted to know exactly how the safe had been opened. The thought of a man filing his nails to the quick and then filing until the nerves were exposed bothered him. He had a dozen questions to ask.

"I should think he could have taken an easier way," he said.

"Suppose he had sandpapered the ball of his fingers? It would be less cruel, do you think it would be as effective? Did it seem to pain him? He must

be a fellow of enormous grit. B-r-r-r! I couldn't
do it even if it would open the bars of our little private hell here. What is Dick Price like? What
gave him the idea in the beginning?"

I was amazed at his gossipy quizzing.

"Hell, man, you must be first cousin to the Spanish
Inquisition," I rallied. "Why are you so much interested?"

"Colonel, this is a wonderful episode," he said. "It
will make a great story."

I had not thought of it in such a light. Bill's
mind was ever on the alert. It was like some wizard
camera with the lens always in focus. Men, their
thoughts and their doings, were snapped in its tireless eye.

All life, as he tells us in "The Duplicity of Har-
graves," belonged to him. He took thereof what he
pleased and returned it as he would.

Once he had taken it, it was his. He stored it
up in his mind. When he called upon it, it came
forth bearing the stamp of his own originality.

Bill took no notes. Once in a while he would jot
a word or two down on a scrap of paper, a corner
of a napkin, but in all of our rambles together I
never noticed the pencil much in evidence. He preferred to work his unfailing memory.

It seemed to have boundless space for his multi-
tudinous ideas. He kept them mentally pigeonholed
and tabulated, ready to be taken out and used at a
moment's notice. It was years before he made Dick
Price immortal in the story of Jimmy Valentine. I
asked him why he had not used it before.

"I've had it in mind, colonel, ever since you told me of it," he answered. "But I was afraid it would not go. Convicts, you know, are not accepted in the best society even in fiction."

Porter had never met Dick Price. One night I brought them together in the warden's office. It was odd to note the instantaneous sympathy between these two unapproachable men.

Both held aloof from the other prisoners; Dick because he was moody, Bill because of his reticence. And yet, between the two there seemed to spring up an immediate understanding.

Porter had brought over a new magazine. He was privileged to receive as many as he liked. He handed it to Dick. The fellow looked up, a glance of wistful swiftness darting across his flushed face.

"I've hardly seen one since I've been here," he said, snatching it quickly and sticking it under his coat. Porter did not understand. When Dick left, I told him what his sentence had been—that he could not receive a book, a visit or even a letter.

"Colonel, do they starve a man's soul and kill his mind like that?" He said nothing more. He seemed shocked and bitter. In a moment he got up to go. At the door he turned.

"Well for him that he has not much longer to live."

The words sent a gust of white fury over me. I began to fear again. I went over to the ranges every night to see Dick. He was getting worse. I begged the warden to press his case.

At last the day came when the Governor was to

pass upon it. There was nothing for him to do but to sign it. Dick had performed his part of the bargain. The State could now pay off its obligation. I told Dick.

"You can have a nice little feed with the old woman day after tomorrow," I said. He didn't answer. He didn't want me to know he hoped, but in spite of himself his breath came hurriedly and he turned his back quickly.

I knew then that this silent, grateful fellow had been waiting and counting on that pardon. I knew that the thought of freedom and a few years of peace had sustained him in all the suffering of these last months.

The next morning I got the word from the warden. The pardon had been denied.

When the warden gave me that word I felt as though a black wall had dropped suddenly before me, cutting off the light and the air. I felt shut-in, smothered, dumb.

What would poor Dick do now? What would he think of me? If I had not told him it was coming up I might have jollied him along. But he knew. He would be waiting for me. All day he would be thinking of it. I would have to see him in the corridors that night.

When I went into his range, there he was, pacing up and down the corridor. I looked at the stooped, emaciated form. The prison clothes hung from his bones as though he were a peg. His haggard face turned upon me a look of such pathetic eagerness I felt my courage sinking in a cold, speechless misery.

I tried to tell him. The words got caught in the gulp in my throat.

The flush faded from his dark cheek until his skin looked the color of a gray cinder, with the over-brilliant eyes glaring forth like burning coals. He understood. He stood there staring at me like a man who has heard his own death sentence. And I could not say a word to him. After a moment, age-long with its dull agony, he put out his hand.

"It's all right, Al," his voice was a choking whisper. "I don't care. Hell, it doesn't make any difference to me."

But it did. It finished him. It broke his heart. He hadn't the courage to fight it out any longer. A month later they took him to the prison hospital.

He was dying. There was no chance of a cure. I wanted to write to his old mother. But it would only have pained her. They wouldn't have let her come to him. The warden couldn't break the State's law. So I just went to see him every few nights. I sat and talked to him. As I would come up to his cot he would put out his hand and grin. And when I looked into those quick, intelligent, game eyes, a stab of pain went through me. He never spoke of his old mother now.

At this time I was a somewhat privileged character in the prison. As the warden's secretary, I could visit any department at will. Otherwise Dick Price might have died and I would never have had even one chance to see him.

When a convict went to the hospital he was cut off from all communication with his former fellows.

Men lay sometimes for months in their cots without ever a word from the only friends they had. They suffered and died without one touch of human sympathy.

I was the only visitor Dick had. Men had called him a "stir bug" because of his erratic, moody ways—because, too, of his uncanny genius as a mechanic. As he lay there coughing his life away, he was the gentlest and the calmest soul in the prison. He viewed his suffering and his certain death as a spectator might have. The queerest, oddest fancies possessed him. One night he turned to me with a whimsical dreaminess in his voice.

"Al, why do you suppose I was born?" he asked. "Would you say that I had ever lived?"

I couldn't think of any answer to make. I knew that I had lived and got a lot of joy out of it. I wasn't sure about Dick. He didn't wait for my verdict.

"Remember that book your friend Bill slipped me? I read every story in it. It showed me just how I stack up. It told me what a real life might mean. I'm 36 years old and I'm dying without ever having lived. Look at this, Al."

He handed me a scrap of paper with a long list of short phrases on it.

"Those are the things I've never done. Think of it, Al. I never saw the ocean, never sang, never danced, never went to a theatre, never saw a good painting, never said a real prayer——

"Al, do you know that I never talked to a girl in my life? Never had one of them so much as give me a kind look? I'd like to figure out why I was born."

There came a week when I was so busy I did not go to see him. One night very late I dropped into the post-office to talk to Billy Raidler. Down the alley toward the dead house came the big negro porter, whistling and shuffling along. Billy and I used to look out, inquire the name of the stiff, and pay no further respects. We were familiar with death and suffering. This night the negro rapped at the window.

"Massa Al, can't nebber guess who I'se got with me to-night?"

"Who, Sam?" we called out.

"Little Dick Price."

Little Dick, thrown into the wheelbarrow, with nothing but an old rag over his body, his head lopped out at one end, his feet hung over the other. Sam rattled the barrow off to the dead house.

I stayed with Billy that night. Both of us were fond of Dick. We couldn't sleep. Billy sat up in bed.

" 'Sleep, Al?" he called.

"Hell, no."

"God, don't it give you the creeps to think of poor little Dick alone down there in that trough?"

I went down to the dead house the next morning. Dick was already closed up in the rough wooden box. The one-horse spring wagon that carried off the unclaimed convict dead was waiting to take him to the potter's field. I was the only one who followed him. The wagon started off at a trot. I ran ahead of it to the east gate. Old Tommy, the gate-man, stopped me.

"What you after, Mr. Al?"

"I'm just coming as far as I can with a friend of mine," I told him.

The gate swung to. It was a chill, foggy morning. I looked out. Leaning against a tree was a poor, huddled, bent little figure, with an old red shawl drawn tight about the shoulders. She had her hands clasped tight together, her elbows dug into her waist, and she was swinging those hands up and down and shaking her head in a grief so abject, so desolate, it sent a broken sob even into old Tommy's voice.

"Tommy, go speak to her," I said. "That's Dick's mother."

"Aw, gee, ain't that hell! The poor old soul!"

The spring wagon rattled by. Tommy put up his hand to the driver. "Go slow there, ye heartless boob. That there is the poor lad's old mother."

The driver reined in the horse. Dick's mother lurched against the wagon and looked in at the wooden box. She was swaying from side to side like a crazy thing.

All that she had on earth—the boy whose tragic, broken life had been her crucifixion—was in that crude box. The wagon jogged off—the trembling, heart-piercing old figure half running, half falling along the road after it.

Society had taken the last farthing of its debt from Dick Price and it had beaten his mother into the dust in the cruel bargain.

CHAPTER XX.

The Prison Demon; the beast exhibited; magic of kindness; reclamation; tragedy of Ira Maralatt; meeting of father and daughter.

Such is the story of Jimmy Valentine as it unfolded itself in the Ohio penitentiary. O. Henry takes the one great episode in that futile life and with it he wins the tears and the grateful smiles of the nation. In that throbbing silence, when the ex-con opens the safe and the little sister of the girl he loves is saved from suffocation, Jimmy as he might have been, not Jimmy as he was, is before us. Few who have breathed hard in that gripping moment would have denied Dick Price his chance, would have refused him the pardon he earned, would have doomed him to his forlorn and lonely death in the prison hospital.

Bill Porter was not the grim artist to paint that harsh picture for the world. He loved a happy ending. He could not even give the exact details of the safe-opening. It was too cruel for his light and winsome fancy.

That was ever Bill's way. He took the facts, but he twisted them as he would. I asked him about it later. In the story he gives the hero a costly set of tools wherewith to open the vault. He does not have him file his nails.

"Colonel, it chills my teeth to think of that gritting operation," he said. "I prefer the set of tools. I don't like to make my victims suffer. And then, you see, the tools enable Jimmy to make a present to a friend. That gift illustrates the toleration of the man who has been in prison.

"Jimmy decided to quit the game himself, but he does not expect the whole world to share his fervor of reform. Instead of burying the instruments of his former profession, as your reformed citizen would have done, he straightway sends them to a former pal. I like that spirit in my character.

"The ordinary man who makes a New Year's resolution immediately sends down censure on the fellow who isn't perched on the wagon with him. Jimmy does no such thing. That's one of the advantages of spending a few vacations in prison. You grow mellow in your judgments."

This soft, golden toleration was one of the gracious traits in Porter's character. It won him friends even though his aloof dignity forbade familiarity. In the "pen" he was universally respected. The meanest cutthroat in the ranges felt honored to serve him.

Porter's "drag" with the prison barber was the subject of raillery at the club. The barber was an artist in his trade. He seemed to take a mean delight in turning out grotesque, futuristic patterns in headdress. But for Porter the most exquisite precision was observed. His thin, yellow hair was trimmed to a nicety. The kind, easy manner of the man had completely captivated, the burly-hearted convict barber.

If it had not been for this humorous, penetrative understanding in Porter, the Recluse Club would not have endured a month. He was its equilibrium. Many a violent clash ended in a laugh because of an odd fling Bill Porter would interject into the turmoil.

Men who have been walled off from free contact with their fellows become excessively quarrelsome and "touchy." We were cooped together like children in an over-large family. We had no escape from each other's society.

The isolation of prison life whets antagonism. Men who could travel to the ends of the earth in friendship would, in a sudden raging bitterness, spring like tigers at each other's throat. Even in the happiness of our Sunday dinners these explosive outbursts would break out among the members.

It would start with the merest trifle, and all at once there would be fiercely angry taunts flung from one to the other. In one of these uncalled for eruptions I sent in my resignation to the club.

Billy Raidler had protested that he could taste the soapsuds on the dishes. I was the chief dishwasher. I did not like the imputation. I would not have minded Billy's protest, but old man Carnot backed him up with further criticism.

"Most assuredly we can taste the soap," he said. "But worse than that, I do not like the garlic. Now, Mr. Jennings, why can you not pick the odious vegetable out of the roast?"

Carnot was an irascible old epicure. He wanted his napkin folded oblong and his knife and fork laid down in a certain fashion. He never failed to resent the introduction of the garlic Louisa loved.

Every one at the table took up the issue. They could all taste the soapsuds, they said. "Damn' pigs, all of you! Take the honor at the dishpan yourselves." I was furious with resentment. I could have hurled the pots and skillets at them. The next Sunday I did not go to the club. I told Billy I was finished with them. Billy had no patience with the sulks and left me in a huff.

Porter came over to the post-office and knocked at the door. "Colonel," he said, and there was such understanding indulgence in his tone I felt immediately appeased, "don't you think you better reconsider?"

"You're the very salt of the earth. The club is absolutely flat without your presence. You see, we only agreed with Billy to sustain him. He's a cripple. He can't stand alone."

It was just the sort of pampering to mollify unreasonable hot temper. Porter was always ready to smooth us down. He was always ready to hear our grievances. His own troubles he bore alone.

Whenever he did reveal his thoughts it was by an accidental outcropping in a lightsome talk. He and Louisa used to indulge in long discussions on astronomy and evolution. Porter was facetious, Louisa serious and very scientific. Louisa would be mixing up a gravy or a sauce.

"You're something of a little creator in the culinary line, Louisa," Porter would say. "What do you suppose were the ingredients used in the creation of the world?"

Louisa's attention was instant. He would talk

about protoplasm and the gradual accommodation of living organism to environment.

"Tut, tut," Porter would mock. "I hold fast to the Biblical story. What else should men be made of but a handful of mud? The Creator was right; men are but dirt. Take Ira Maralatt, the Prison Demon, for instance."

A queer, yellowish pallor spread over Bill's face. I knew that the name had slipped from Porter's lips unconsciously.

"Colonel, it is a ghastly thing to see a man degraded into a beast like Maralatt," he said. "Last night they beat him to strips again. I had to go down to the basement to sponge him off. I tell you it would take a floor mop to do the job right—he is such a giant."

It was the first time I had ever heard Porter speak of Maralatt, the Prison Demon, yet he had perhaps to sponge him off two or three times a week. Maralatt was the untamed tiger of the "stir." He was the prison horror. He had attacked and stabbed a dozen guards.

For fourteen years he had been in solitary, practically buried alive in the black hole in the basement without a bed, without blankets, without light.

When the guards would attempt to clean out the cell Ira would spring at them. They would overpower him, beat him and hang him up by the wrists. Still he was unsubdued. He kept the prison in recurring spasms of fright.

No one knew who would be his next victim. He was as ferocious as a mad bull.

I had never seen him. Porter's exclamation filled me with curiosity. I went over the next evening to ask him about Maralatt. We were standing in one of the wards just above the punishment cell.

A sudden wild, terrific scream, tortured and agonized, split the air. There was a frenzied scuffle, a booming thud, and a guard's voice shrilled out in frantic terror.

Porter's tranquil face quivered. "Maralatt," he whispered. "Murder at last!"

The next morning excitement shot like a flash from face to face. A big secret was out. Maralatt had nearly strangled a guard the night before. He was to be moved from his dungeon in solitary to a steel cage built in solid stone at the end of the east corridor.

For months they had been building the cage. It was a revolting thing, made as if to house some ferocious jungle beast. It opened into a niche in the stone about four by eight feet. In the niche Ira was to sleep.

We got the tip from the warden's office. I had been sent on a message across the campus. I came into the alley-like corridor, passing a few guards. A look of riven terror held them staring and silent. Their frightened eyes were fastened on the door that led to the solitary cells.

The door sprang open, and a spectacle to freeze the heart with its terrific and grisly horror was before us. I saw the Prison Demon. Hulk-shouldered, gigantic, lurched forward, he towered above the dozen guards like a huge, ferocious gorilla-man.

I could see his face. The hair was matted about him, the clothes torn in ragged strips.

The guards stood at a distance, pushing him forward with long poles. They stood on either side. The demon could not escape. At the ends of the poles were strong iron hooks, fastened into his flesh, and as the guards pushed the hooks jagged into the prisoner's bones. He was compelled to walk.

On his foot was the monstrous Oregon boot. Every step must have been an agony. There was no sound from the Prison Demon. Across the grass to the new-made dungeon in the old A and B block the hellish procession took its way. Ira Maralatt was riveted to his steel cage and a sign, "Prison Demon," pasted above the grating.

The Prison Demon became an attraction at the penitentiary. His fame spread over the city—almost over the State. He was known as the brute man—the hell fiend. Visitors wanted a sight of him. The old warden saw a chance to turn a penny. For 25 cents citizens were taken down the east corridor and allowed to stare at the degraded thing that had once been a man.

Ira was not a willing party to the bargain. He had a mean habit of crouching down in the far corner of his black cage and cheating the visitors of their money's worth. One day a distinguished citizen stood in the alley half an hour waiting for the demon to exhibit himself. Threats and prods from the guards were fruitless. The matter was reported to the warden. Incensed and blustering, he came running down the corridor.

"Open the door," he called to one of the guards. No one moved. They did not dare obey the order.

"Open the door," Coffin yelled, snatching the club from one of the guards. He sprang into the cage, the club raised, rushing furiously toward the crouching giant in the corner.

"Come out, you fiend!" he bawled. The Demon reared, hurled himself upright and lunged with the violence of a raging Colossus against the warden. The sudden mad impact bowled the warden over.

Ira snatched the club and flung it forth for a crashing blow on Coffin's head. Two guards dashed into the cage, caught Ira by the feet and sent him thundering backward against the wall.

The visitor got his 25 cents' worth that day.

The warden's escape was little short of a miracle. It taught him a lesson. He devised a safer scheme for bringing Maralatt out of his wretched hole. From a window in the inner hall he had a hose attached to the cage. It would send down a storming current of ice-cold water that would cut the flesh of the cowering Demon.

Ira would come roaring like an infuriated lion to the bars of the cage. He would grab the steel in his mighty hands, shaking it, and filling the alley with wild, maniac screams.

This practice continued two or three months. The new warden came in, took down the sign from Ira's cage and prevented the shameful exhibits.

The sequel to Ira's tragic history came many months later, after I had been appointed private secretary to Warden W. N. Darby. Darby had a kind, magnificent sympathy in his enthusiastic nature. He had an eager ear for suggestions, even from the meanest convict. A chance incident opened the dark book of Ira Maralatt's ghastly life.

One evening I was walking down the east corridor on my way to the asylum. I had taken an apple from the warden's table where I ate. I was bringing the fruit to a poor fellow in the prison "bughouse." He had lost his mind and his eyesight in the hoe polishing shop. The hoes were polished on emery wheels.

Millions of steel particles darted about, often puncturing the convicts in the face and neck. The sparks had gotten this poor devil in the forehead and eyes. I used to bring him an extra bit to eat.

As a I passed the prison demon's cage I caught a glimpse of a haggard face at the low opening into the stone cell. Like a dumb, pathetic apparition, wretched and uncertain, the lumbering figure groped from corner to corner. The red, sunken eyes seemed to be burning deep into the smeared and pallid cheeks.

One hand that was but a mammoth yellow claw was pressed against the rough mat of black hair. More like a hurt and broken Samson than like a hell fiend Ira Maralatt looked as his eye met mine in startled fear.

Something in the defenseless misery of his glance held me. I ran back to his cage, took the apple from my pocket, pressed it through the bars, rolling it over to Maralatt. He drew back. I called softly to him.

"There's an apple for you, Ira." He made no answer. I stepped into a shadow in the corridor and waited.

In a moment I saw the huge creature creeping stealthily forward on his hands and knees. The great yellow claw reached out. The broken cuff and link on his arm clanked on the cement. The chain was imbedded into his wrist and the flesh bulged out over it. The hand closed over the apple. The Demon leaped back to his corner.

After that I felt myself drawn to the Prison Demon's cage. Ira no longer seemed a fiend to me, but an abused and tormented human. I sat outside his cell and called to him. He must have recognized my voice, for he came creeping with a hunching swiftness to the front of the cage. He always went on all fours.

"Did you like the apple, Ira?" He looked up at me, as though a thought were struggling in his mind. He did not answer, but sat there watching me. Then he shook his shaggy head and crept back to the stone niche.

I thought I would ask Bill Porter about him. Whenever Ira had been beaten Bill, as the hospital attendant, had been called in to revive him. The theme nauseated Porter. The memory of the raw and bleeding flesh he had so many times sponged sent a shudder of revulsion through him.

"Don't speak of it. This place becomes more unendurable each moment. I try to write in the night. Some wretch, racked with unbearable pain, screams out. It goes like a cold blade to the throat. It comes into my story like a death rattle in the midst of a wedding. Then I can work no longer."

"But you saw Ira and watched him more than others. Is he a demon?"

"Colonel, the man should be in an insane asylum, not in a prison. There's something pressing on his brain. That's my opinion.

I felt satisfied with the verdict. Every night I used to go down to Ira's cage, bringing him pieces of biscuit or meat from the warden's table. In a little while I knew that Ira counted on these visits. I would find him waiting for me.

This wild man, who had become a thing of terror with his hand against his fellows, would be sitting close to the bars, his glowing, uncomprehending eyes peering with a glance of cringing supplication for my coming.

He would take the biscuits from my hands and eat them before me. For fourteen years no one had ever seen the Prison Demon eat. His food would be shoved through the grating. He would not touch it. In the night he would drag it into his cell.

We would talk about the prison. Ira could answer intelligently. Then I would try to draw his history from him. I could hardly ever get more than three or four words. He couldn't remember. He would point to his head and press his hand against it.

We knew that Ira was in for murder, that he had choked a man to death. No one knew the circumstances leading to the crime. No one had ever cared. I thought I would send a letter to some friends if he had any. They might help him.

"Don't know. Head hurts," he would answer in a guttural indistinct voice. "Got a lick on the head once. Coal car hit me.

Night and night, after the most laborious pauses, he would give me the same answers. He wanted to remember. When he failed he would press his powerful hands together and turn to me in abject, appealing despair. But once he seemed to have a gleam of recollection.

I became absorbed in piecing together the solitary words he muttered. I must have been sitting there half an hour. A runner from the warden came shouting down the main corridor for me.

"Where in hell have you been serenading?" Darby thundered. On a quick impulse I told him of the demon and the apple.

"Ira's only a poor demented creature. He got a lick on the head once. He's harmless as an infant if you handle him right."

Darby looked at me as though I were mad.

"It's a fact. He eats out of my hand."

"If that's true then I'll take him out of there."

We went down the next morning to the cage. The warden ordered the door opened. I could see the dark outlines of Ira's figure. The guard was frightened. Darby took the key, turned the lock and stepped forward. If he had suddenly flung himself under a moving engine, death would not have seemed more certain. Ira drew back, hesitated, then leaped with all his mighty bulk toward Darby.

"Ira!" I shouted. The massive figure stiffened as though an electric voltage had suddenly gone through him. The Prison Demon dropped his arm to the ground and came creeping toward me.

"Be good, Ira," I whispered.

The warden braced himself. We went into the tiny cell room. The stench and filth of the hole came up like a sickening wave against us. "Come outside, Ira," the warden said. I nodded. "If I give you a good job, Ira, will you behave?"

It was the first time Ira had heard a kind word from a prison official. He looked about, his eyes narrowing distrustfully, and began to edge away from the warden.

"He'll treat you square, Ira."

The towering giant could have crushed me in his two hands. He was about a foot taller than I, but he shuffled along at my side, looking down at me with a meek docility that filled the guards with wonder.

The warden made straight for the hospital, ordered good food and skilled attention for the Demon. Three weeks later the Ohio penitentiary had a soft-tongued Hercules in the place of the insensate beast that had been Ira Maralatt. The doctors had found the skull pressing on the brain, operated and removed the "dent" that had sent Ira into his mad fits of murderous, unreasoning rage. Memory returned to him. Ira told a story, moving and compelling in its elemental tragedy.

He had been an iron puddler in the steel mills of Cleveland. Before a furnace, vast and roaring as a hell pit, the half-nude puddler works, stirring the molten iron. He breathes in a red hot, blasting hurricane. He moves in a bellowing clamor louder than the shout of a thousand engines. Only the strongest can withstand the deafening tumult, the scorching air of that bedlam. Ira Maralatt was one of these.

There came a strike in the mills. Ira went home to his wife. He had been married but a year. They had been paying down on a little home. Ira could get no work. The walkout dashed their hopes.

"I'm going to Canaltown, to the mines," he told the girl-wife one day. "I'll be back as soon as it's settled." She walked with him to the gate. He never saw her again. When Ira returned to the little home all that had been dear and sacred to him was gone.

In West Virginia Maralatt got a job in the coal mines. He was working near one of the pillars. A coal car shot along the tracks to the chutes to be filled. The car with its tonnage started down the grade.

Just at the pillar it should have switched. Instead, it came heading straight toward Ira. Further down the track twenty men were working. The car, with the tremendous speed of the runaway, would have crushed them to a pulp.

There was one chance of escape for them. Ira took it. The gigantic hands went out, caught the bolting car and with a smashing force sent the top-heavy four-wheeler sideways.

In the terrible impact Ira caromed against the wall of the mine. The lives of twenty men were saved. The mashed and unconscious form of the gigantic Maralatt was dragged out and sent to the hospital.

Without a thought of himself and his own life, Ira Maralatt had hurled himself across the path of the runaway coal car. If he had died his fellows would have exalted the memory of the man whose splendid courage had saved twenty lives. Ira lived —but the sacrifice took a dearer thing than mere existence. It gave him not honor, but a shameful brand. He became the Prison Demon.

After the tragic disaster in the coal mine, Ira lay for months in the hospital. He was finally sent out as cured.

The strike at the steel mills had been settled. Back to Cleveland and the little home the iron puddler went.

There was a pathway, hedged with cowslips, leading up to the door. Ira walked quickly, meaning to surprise the wife who had not heard from him in the months he had been at the hospital.

There were new curtains at the window. A hand rustled muslin drapery aside. A strange face looked with doubtful question on the man at the hedge.

"Good morning, sir," the woman said.

"Good morning, indeed," Maralatt answered, mystified and startled.

"Who lives here?"

"What's that to you?" the woman snapped.

"This is my home and my wife's!" Suddenly excited and trembling, Ira turned upon the strange woman.

"Where is my wife?" Where is Dora Maralatt?"

"Oh, her! She's gone. I don't know where. Got put out. Are you the missing husband?" the woman sneered. "Well, there's your bag and baggage over in the lot there!" With a laughing shrug, she pushed the curtain to its place.

Over in the lot, dumped out like a rubbish heap, Maralatt found the remnants of his home. There was the chest with the wrought-steel corners he had given Dora for a birthday gift—there was the dining-room table and the six chairs that had been the pride of the girl's heart. There, too, was a thing Ira had never seen before—a clothes basket tied with pink stuff and ribbons.

Distracted, enraged, like one suddenly demented, he ran back to the cottage door and banged on the panel.

"Go away from here with your noise," the woman called. "I'll have you arrested!"

"Open the door," Maralatt stormed, "please, I'll not come in. Open it just a moment. My wife, did you see her go? Is she alive? Tell me just that. How long is she gone? Where can she be?"

The woman softened. "Don't get so excited and I'll tell you. She went out alive. But she was pretty well done in. She looked about gone. I don't know where she went. Maybe she's dead now."

"The baby—did it die, too?"

"I don't know about that. She left before it was born. "Well, now, I'm sorry for you, poor fellow, but I don't know where she is. I'll tell you—you might go down to the landlord. He knows. He's the one that ordered those things dumped out. He's down at the same old office."

Before the words were out of her mouth Maralatt bolted down the path, tearing like a wild man through the streets. "Where's my wife?" Where's Dora Maralatt? Where's the girl you put out of the bungalow on the hill?"

In a rushing fury the questions tumbled from his lips. The agent looked at him with contemptuous insult. "Who let this maniac into the office? Throw him out?"

The order calmed Maralatt. He leaned forward, touching the man's hand. "Excuse me, I'm a bit excited. I've been away. You know me, don't you? I was buying that little cottage on C street. I've been sick. I came back. I can't find my wife. Could you tell me where she is? They say you put her out."

"Oh, you're the missing puddler! Well, you've lost the house. Yes, the woman was put out. I remember it all now. She made a fuss about it. We had to throw her out."

"Where is she?" Maralatt was breathing quick and short in a choking panic. "Where's my wife gone?"

"Oh, get out of here! The house is lost. What do I care about your wife. Why didn't you stick around and look after her?"

"Well, you put her out, didn't you? Where did she go to?"

"The damn' scrub's in hell, where she ought to be! Who cares about your ——— of a wife anyway! Get out of here!"

The balance slipped. A blood-crazed panther, Maralatt, leaped over the counter, "My what of a

wife! What—what—what—you damned scoundrel!
My wife—what? Say it again! You thief, you vil-
lain, say it again!"

Iron hands swooped the agent from the floor,
wrenching the neck as though it were but a chicken's.
Back and forth until the skin on the scarlet cheeks
was like to burst, Maralatt knocked that grasping
head. It took three officers to break those hands
loose from the dead man's throat.

A foaming maniac, Maralatt was knocked insen-
sible, thrown into the patrol wagon, and taken off to
the station house.

His mind was gone. He was sent up for life to the
Ohio penitentiary. No defense had been made for
him.

This was the story Ira told the warden after the
operation at the prison hospital had restored his
memory. The giant Hercules was no longer a gorilla
man. Clean, quiet, spent, he sat like a kind old
patriarch and told the aching tale.

Darby made him caretaker in the condemned row.
Ira cleaned out the cells, swept the room where the
electric chair was kept and took the food to these convicts. Doomed men, counting the days between
them and the chair, played checkers with the prison
demon now. In the ghastly fear of the nightmare
days before execution many a lost unfortunate found
comfort in the benediction of Maralatt's sympathetic
presence.

I used to visit Ira in the condemned row. He was
happy and serene. Some one had given him a pair
of canary birds. The warden allowed him to raise

them in his cell. First he had four, then ten, before long the dull, clamorous silence of the doomed men was filled with the joyous, thrilling song of many canary birds.

It was a touching thing to see the white-haired giant sitting in his cell—the sunlight coming in in golden radiance through the window in the inner wall, and these yellow fluttering, singing things perched on his shoulders and resting in the palms of his great hands.

Dark faces pressed against the bars of the condemned cells. "Ira, bring me a bird, let me hold it a moment!" one would call. "Ira, have Melba sing the "Toreador," another would grimly jest. In the near approach of their death, Ira and his birds and his gentle ministrations were like a prophecy of living hope.

One day Warden Darby hurried into the office. He had been up to Cleveland. His voice was brusque. "I have discovered something," he said. "Send for Ira Maralatt, at once."

"Sit down, Ira, and be calm." The warden could scarcely suppress the emotion of his own voice. "I've been up to Cleveland. Ran into the strangest thing. Guess you told a straight story, all right!"

"Yes, sir," Ira answered, a frightened light in his eye. "Yes, sir it was the truth. Leastways, I'm pretty sure it was. Surely, I couldn't have dreamed it, could I?"

"Now, that's all right. But listen to me. You had a wife, you say? Dora, that was her name, wasn't it? Well, she died—died right after they put her out of the cottage. The baby lived. She's alive today. I met her. She's pretty. She was adopted by wealthy people here in Columbus. They're friends of the governor. I just happened to talk about you. The girl's foster mother is a relative of your wife's. She thought you were a maniac. I told her the truth.

"Ira, go over to the State shop, get a suit and shoes. You're pardoned. I took it up with the Governor. You go out tomorrow.

With a shock of bewildered emotion that sent a quiver of sobbing happiness into his voice, Ira Maralatt put out his hands to the warden.

"Does the girl know?"

"Now, no, they haven't told her. It would be too sudden a strain."

The next morning Ira, in his cheap suit, the squeaky prison shoes and a light straw hat, came to the warden's office. His gigantic frame was stooped and his face shot through with nervous excitement.

"You did all this, Mr. Al," he said, the tears crowding into his eyes. "Just think what you did when you rolled that apple to me." He hesitated a moment. "Mr. Al, she won't ever recognize me, will she? I don't think I'd like her to know her father was the Prison Demon."

When Darby handed him the pardon and the five dollars his hands shook. "I don't know how to thank you, warden!"

"You don't have to—God knows you've paid for it!"

Ira took two of his little canaries with him. "I'll give them to the girl for a present. I want to see her. I have to see her." He shook hands with Darby and me.

A week passed. We heard no word from him. The warden became alarmed. "I wonder if anything could have happened to the old man?" Maralatt was but 46. His terrible suffering during 18 years in prison had broken even his magnificent strength. He seemed about 60. "I wonder if he went to see his daughter? Funny, I didn't hear."

It worried Darby so much he inquired. He sent for the girl's foster mother. He told her of Ira and the canaries. Back came the frantic answer from the daughter herself. In an hour she was at the warden's office.

"An old man with canaries?" Yes, an old man had come with them. She had the birds now. "What about it? That man, my father!"

"Why didn't some one tell me? How dare they keep it from me. That's what he meant when he left. That's why he called me little Dora. Oh, what shall we do now?"

In broken sentences she told of the mysterious visit of the old bird-peddler. Ira had gone up the steps of the palatial home where the girl lived. He had brought the little cage with the birds. Perhaps he had intended to tell Mary he was her father. The sight of her beauty, her culture, her happiness had chilled his ardor. The grand old fellow could not bear to spoil her glad youth with the tragedy of his bleak life. He had left with his claim unspoken.

The girl was coming down the stairs as the old man rang the bell. The butler had denied him entrance. And the girl had run forward and ordered the old man to come in.

"I thought, Miss, perhaps you would buy these birds. I'm poor and they are wonderful singers. I raised them myself."

And just out of sympathy for the pathetic old stranger, the girl had bought the canaries. He would only take a dollar from her. She had not understood. He had looked at her and the tears had streamed down his cheeks.

"Good-by, little Dora," he said as he left. He stood at the door as though he were about to say something further and then he looked at her with a queer, sad light on his face and went down the steps.

They thought he was a harmless, unbalanced old oddity.

"Where can I find him? Where shall I look for him? Why didn't some one tell me?" the girl was torn with grief. "Hurry, let us look now."

Outside it was snowing. There had been a wind storm for a week. Maralatt's daughter and the warden searched in every street and alley for the old man. He was nowhere to be found.

One night there was a knock at the guard-room door and a faint voice called out, "Let me come in, please." The captain of the guard opened the door. Ira Maralatt, his thin prison suit drenched and hanging in a limp rag about him, was kneeling in the snow at the prison door.

"Let me in, please, I have nowhere to go."

"No, no, go away, you're pardoned. I can't let you in, it's against the law," the captain answered.

The warden was informed.

"Who was it?" he asked.

"Maralatt," they answered.

He came rushing to the gate and ordered it opened. Maralatt was not there.

Darby swore at them.

"Don't you know we've been looking everywhere for him for weeks?"

Beyond the walls, flinging himself along, the warden went on the search. He came back fifteen minutes later, the half-frozen Maralatt limping along at his side. He found him down in the snow near the river. Ira was burning up with fever. His face was already stricken with death.

Everywhere he went asking for work, he said, they had refused him. They said he was too old. Finally he gave up trying.

The warden sent for Maralatt's daughter.

The young girl, graceful and white as an angel, flung herself into the old man's arms.

"Don't die, daddy! Why didn't you tell me? See, I'm your girl, Mary. Just look at me! Oh, why didn't I know? If you only knew how many times I longed for a father—any one, any kind. Why didn't you tell me?"

Maralatt looked at her in dim, feverish gladness. He took the delicate hands in his gigantic palm and turned to her.

"I looked all over for you, Mary," he said. "I'm so glad you came."

With a smile of wondrous peace on his lips, the prison demon sank back on the pillows. The old hero had won his palm at last.

CHAPTER XXI.

Methods of O. Henry; his promotion; the singing of Sally Castleton; O. Henry's indifference; the explanation.

The shadows of a thousand Dick Prices and Ira Maralatts skulked like unhappy ghosts through the cell corridors of the Ohio penitentiary. The memory of a thousand tragedies seemed to abide in the very air of the ranges. Men who allowed themselves to come under the persistent gloom of these haunting presences went mad.

The rest of us sought an outlet in gayety—in a hundred trivial little incidents that would bring a laugh out of all proportion to their funniness. In self-defense, the convict becomes hardened to the brutal suffering of the life about him.

If any one had heard Billy Raidler, Bill Porter and me, as we talked and guffawed in the prison post-office, he would have rated us an unthinking trio of irresponsible scamps.

We never aired our melancholy, but we would wrangle and jest by the hour over the probable course a fly batting itself against the post-office window might take if we let it out—over the origin of the black race and the finish of the Caucasian family.

Or we would imagine that the prison was suddenly crushed to pieces in an earthquake, and we would begin to speculate on the menace of our presence to a terror-stricken society. No subject was too ridiculous to beguile an hour away.

Porter was not supposed to visit the post-office while he was on duty at the hospital. As he never violated any of the prison rules, he always made it a point to come on business. Billy Raidler was a semi-invalid, and offered an unfailing excuse. Billy's amber hair was falling out. He hounded Porter to bring him a remedy.

"Look here, Bill," the ex-train robber would say, "if you could get the arsenic out of that rock-ribbed old Coffin why can't you rouse the hair that ought to be on my scalp?"

Warden Coffin, by some mistake, had been given an overdose of arsenic. Antidotes failed. Porter was called in. He saved the life of Coffin. This incident happened before my arrival at the "pen," but Raidler never gave Porter any peace about it. Porter always maintained that the warden was dying of fright, not of the arsenic. He said his antidote was "simplicity."

"Simplicity or duplicity," Raidler countered, "you interfered with the ways of Divine Providence, Bill, when you saved Coffin's life. Now come through and give the archduke a helping hand. Put a little fertilizer on this unirrigated thatch of mine."

So Porter came over one day, looking very important and complacent. One short, fat hand was stuck in his vest and in the other he carried a glove. Porter was an unmitigated dandy, even in the prison. He liked rich, well-fitting clothes. He abhorred noisy styles or colors. I never saw him when he was not well groomed and neat in his appearance.

"Adonis Raidler," Porter ceremoniously laid the glove on the desk and drew forth a bulky, odorous package, "behold the peerless hair-regenerator compounded after tireless, scientific research by one unredeemed Bill Porter."

Raidler grabbed the bottle and pulled out the cork. The heavy pungence of wintergreen filled the office.

"The scent is in harmony with your esthetic soul, Billy," Porter said. "Elusive fragrance might not reach that olfactory nerve of yours."

Billy doused some of the liquid on his head and beban to rub it viciously in. He had the most child-like faith in Porter's genius as a chemist. Every night after that I went to sleep fairly drugged by the cloud of wintergreen under which Billy submerged himself.

Every morning he would bring over the comb to show me that fewer hairs had come out than the day before. Whatever Billy wanted his hair for, none of us could understand. The hair-restorer was nothing but bum bay rum outraged by an overdose of wintergreen fragrance. Either Porter's patent, Billy's massaging or his faith stopped the emigration of his hair.

"Now that your locks, thanks to my scientific skill, promise to grow as long as a musician's," Porter boasted, "why not get a fife, Billy, and learn to play it? The colonel here will teach you. And then the three of us will set forth from this fortress of mighty stone and like troubadours of old we will go a-minstreling from village to village!"

Porter had a guitar and he picked it with graceful touch. I played the tuba. If Billy could only play the fife, what a joyous troupe we would make!

The idea tickled Porter. He was really in earnest about it. I think his ideal of existence was just such a free vagabondage. Many and many a time in the post-office he had brought up the subject.

"Will you get that fife, Billy?" he said one night. "I have a plan. We will go over and serenade Miles Ogle. If he likes the tufted tinkle of our mellow madness, why forth let us stride to woo the belle demoiselles of all Beautydom!"

Miles Ogle was the greatest counterfeiter in the United States. He was serving a long sentence at the Ohio "pen."

"Would it not be kind to trill forth a gladsome melody to Miles?" Porter's low, whispering voice lent an air of mystery to his lightest comment. I always felt like a conspirator when his hushed tones kept us captive. "Miles, you know, has a wholesome appreciation of the golden note!"

Porter often spoke to me in these later prison days of his serenading in Austin. He said that he belonged to a troupe of singers. "We went about playing and serenading at the windows of all the fair maids in Austin!" Playing, singing, writing a sonnet, sketching a cartoon—what a lovable ne'er-do-well he would have been if this very breezy negligence had not caught him in a net of unfortunate circumstances at the bank.

"I can think of nothing more delightful," he said, "than to strap a harp to my back and saunter from castle to castle living in the gracious beauty of poetry and music.

"We have the dungeon here, but we lack both the drawbridge and the castle. How sweet it would be to sit in the silver moonlight, to summon the fairies from their leafy pavilions with the strains of our warblings! And then to lie back on the grass and weave fantastic dreams to lighten the drab heart of the world!"

Porter was feeling very gay this night. A hope he had silently cherished. As always he came over to share his happiness. He had won an honor craved by every convict in the "stir."

There was a light tap at the post-office door. Billy opened it and took something from the prisoner standing there and softly closed the door. He handed a card to me. In his own handwriting was Bill Porter's name and underneath a drawing of the steward's office.

"Who brought the card?" I asked.

"Bill; he's out there. Shall I let him in?" Raidler was in a whimsical mood. The light tap was repeated. I answered it.

"Gentlemen, why be so exclusive?" Porter walked in with a very pompous air, his shoulders thrown back in an exaggerated swagger. "Permit me to inform you that I have changed my residence. The card will enlighten you as to my present domicile. I moved to-day."

There was a new enthusiasm in his bantering voice. Porter had been appointed secretary to the steward. The position, with the single exception of the secretaryship to the warden, was the best in the pen. It took him beyond the walls. The steward's office was directly across the street from the pen, the edge of the building skirting the river.

"Colonel, you would envy me—" the voice was a low chuckle.

"I have a desk near the window—a big desk with pigeon-holes. I have all the books I want. I can read and think without interruption. Now I can do something."

Seldom had Porter alluded to his ambition to write. We sent out some of his stories, but he let us think they were done just for diversion. The new position gave him plenty of opportunity to try out his talents. He spent every spare moment "practicing," as he used to put it.

We talked about literature and its purposes very often now, for I was even freer than Bill. I had been made secretary to Warden Darby. I had even managed to worm myself out of convict clothes. When I went into Darby's office I was brought into contact with all the distinguished visitors of the State and Nation.

"I look pretty shabby," I hinted to Darby. "I ought to be more up to my position." He turned to me.

"Sure," he said; "go over to the State shop and get the best suit of clothes you can order."

He meant the best suit of convict clothes. I picked out a fine piece of serge and ordered as clever a suit as the Governor might have worn. When Darby saw me without the stripes, he gasped.

"Pretty slick," was the only comment he made. I never wore the stripes again.

Nearly every night Porter would come across the street to visit Billy and me. We would talk by the hour, filling him up on the exploits of bandit days, spinning out the yarns in choice outlaw lingo. He listened captive. The stories seemed to suggest ideas to him. He never used anything just as it was told to him.

"You ought to startle the world," he said to me one day.

"How, by shooting it up?"

"No, colonel, but you have a wonderful lot of stories. You can view life from a thousand viewpoints."

I often wondered at Porter's methods. It seemed to me that he overlooked innumerable stories by his aloofness. He did not seem to have the slightest desire to ferret out the secrets of the men in the pen. The convict as a subject for his stories did not appeal to him.

I am convinced that he felt himself different from the average criminal. It was not until he returned to the world and suffered from its coldness that his sympathies were broadened and his prejudices mellowed.

One very odd experience revealed this trait in Porter. I used to play in the prison band every Sunday at chapel. One morning a song thrilled out from the women's loft.

It was the most magnificent contralto voice I have ever heard. It had a purple depth and intensity of feeling in its tones and at times there was a mournful, piercing pathos in it that struck into the soul like a heartbroken wail.

I looked up, trying to trace the voice to its owner. And finally it seemed to me that a tall, proud looking girl—a Southerner of exceeding beauty—was the singer. Her skin was moon white in its purity, she had splendid gray eyes and hair that fell in a golden radiance about her face. I became greatly interested.

"There's a girl in the pen, Bill," I told Porter, "and you want to come to chapel next Sunday and hear her sing."

"Colonel, I fear you jest. I wouldn't go into the chapel to hear the seven choirs of angels let alone a wretched feminine convict!"

Mrs. Mattie Brown was matron of the women's ward. I was sent over on business. I took the chance to satisfy my curiosity.

"Who is the prima donna that sings on Sundays?" I asked.

"Would you like to see her?" the matron said, looking at me with quiet interest. "You might be able to put in a good word for her and maybe get her a pardon. She's a good girl." Mrs. Brown was always trying to help the women convicts. Her understanding was as warm as the sun and as deep as the sea.

"It's a terrible thing to get it the way she did," the matron said. ' 'She's in on a charge of murder. She got life for it."

The girl came down. She was very slender and the cheap, calico polka-dot dress was out of tone with her rich beauty. She looked like a young queen, whose rags could not conceal her distinction.

As soon as she stood before me I was embarrassed. I did not like to ask her questions, but for once in my life curiosity obsessed me. I told her so.

"Your singing attracted me," I said. "I listen for it every Sunday."

A bitter shadow went like an ugly blot across her face and the girl looked up, her clear eyes marred by their look of self-abasement.

"Sing? Oh, yes; I can sing," the voice that was like amber honey mocked. "I sang myself into hell. I don't mind telling you. It isn't often that anyone is interested enough to listen. My people haven't come near me. They think I disgraced them. Maybe so, I don't care. I haven't seen a soul from the outside in four years. One good thing about prisons, though, you don't live very long in them."

The cynical despondency of this girl, who was not more than 25, robbed me of composure. I couldn't think of a thing to say to her. She was high bred and nervous.

"Isn't it terrible to be scoffed at and have your friends put their hands over their mouths and whisper 'Murderess' when you pass? Oh—I know—" a shudder caught her. "That's what happened to me!" her lips suddenly trembled and her chin shook pitifully. She turned and rushed sobbing down the corridor.

As the girl's rough calico whisked around the corner, the matron shook her head.

"I made a mistake, I shouldn't have brought her down. I didn't think it would affect her so. Now she'll be melancholy for a week. Isn't she a pitiful figure! I wish I could do something for her!"

"Was she guilty?"

"Its pretty hard to say. A man about killed Sally's baby. The man was the baby's father. Sally turned around and shot him through the heart. She's glad about it. I mean she's glad about the killing.

"It was shameful the way her mother and her sisters went back on her. She sat in the court all alone and not a soul was with her when she was condemned. They took her off to the pen as though she were a gutter snipe.

"And Sally had supported that mother and sisters. It was her singing that kept them from starvation."

Sally Castleton was sent up from Hamilton county (Cincinnati) for life. The war had robbed her people of their wealth, but not of their pride. It was more in keeping with their type of dignity to starve than to send their daughters to work.

Sally had a gift in her voice. She sang in the choir of a Cincinnati cathedral. The family managed to exist on what she earned.

The son of a banker in Cincinnati began to attend the services. It was the old tale. He saw Sally. They were both young. The girl was attractive far beyond the measure of average loveliness. They loved.

There were picnics in the suburbs. The banker's son came down to be with Sally. There were rides in a four-in-hand. Old women would run to the windows to catch a glimpse of the handsome banker and the town's beauty. It would be a fine match and an honor to the community.

After a while the banker's son came less and less to Hamilton county. And one night Sally ran away and didn't return.

She went to Cincinnati and got a job in a laundry. She saved up every penny. She never asked aid of anyone.

The matron told me half the story. Sally finished it one day a week later when I met her in the matron's office.

"Why didn't I go to him? Oh—I knew—" Sally clasped her hands. They were delicate as white flowers. "I knew," she went on, after a wistful pause, "he wouldn't want to be bothered. I didn't want to hear him tell me to go away.

"You see, well, as long as I didn't absolutely know what he would say, I could comfort myself imagining that he was thinking of me and wondering what had become of me. I used to lie awake at night. I was too tired to sleep.

"I would see him rushing about the city looking for me. Then he would find me and tell me not to worry —it would be all right. It was easy to console myself.

"But I knew I was fooling myself. I knew he would have turned his back on me. He just changed all at once when he knew. He looked at me with a glance of such disgust and hatred I felt as if a cold frost spread over me. He grabbed up his hat and ran down the walk. Then he turned and came back, and tried to be kind.

" 'Sally, I'll look out for you, I'll come again next Sunday,' he said. I believed him and I waited and waited. I made up excuses for him. But at last I knew that he was never going to come. I couldn't stand the way my mother and sisters looked at me. One night I tied up a few things in a bundle and sneaked out the kitchen door after they were all in bed."

Sally had saved up enough for her expenses. When the baby was a few weeks old she went back to work in the laundry. The old woman where she roomed looked after the little thing. But when it was five or six months old it got sick and Sally had to quit and take care of it.

It was all right as long as the little money lasted. Sally's funds were very small. She gave up eating and spent the money for medicine for the baby. It didn't get any better. She couldn't afford a doctor. She was beside herself with misery.

"If you knew how it looked!" Sally pressed her hands together, her eyes filled with tears. "It had such a dear little white face and the biggest blue eyes. It would turn its head and its poor little mouth would struggle as if it wanted to cry, but was too feeble. It broke my heart to watch it.

"I just got frantic. I used to hold it in my arms, its face pressed against my throat and sometimes I could scarcely feel its breath. I would run up and down the room. I was afraid to look at it for fear it was dying on me.

"Oh, God, you don't know how terrible it is to see the only thing you have in the world just getting weaker and weaker and nothing done to help it. I never slept—I got so I just prayed and prayed to keep it with me.

"And one day it took a spasm. I thought it was gone. I didn't care what I did. I would have crawled in the dust to save it.

"I went to the bank. I waited outside for him. He came down the steps. I followed, waiting until no one was near. Then I edged quietly up to him. 'Phil,' I said.

"He stiffened up as though an electric shock had gone through him. He turned to me in angry contempt, 'What are you dogging me for?'

"It was all I could do to keep from crying. He hurried off and I went stumbling after him. I caught him by the sleeve.

" 'Phil, the baby is dying. I haven't a cent. Oh, I wouldn't let you do anything for it if I could only keep it alive myself. I haven't eaten anything but tea and bread for weeks. And now my last nickel is gone. Phil, will you pay for a doctor for it? It's yours, Phil, your very own. It's the image of you. It has your eyes.'

"For a minute it seemed to me that a look of exultation went across his face. But maybe I imagined it, for he caught my fingers and knocked them off his arm as though I were a leper.

"It does, does it? Well, if it's dying, let it die. I can't keep it alive. Is it my fault if it wants to die?"

"No, no, it's not your fault. But will you help? Will you pay for the doctor—will you help me to take care of it?"

" 'Say, beat it and be damn' quick about it,' he answered. I couldn't believe it. I kept on talking and walking at his side. I don't know what I said. We passed a policeman. He stopped. 'Officer,' he said, 'arrest this rag-picker, will you?'"

They arrested Sally and took her to the Cincinnati jail. The man had sworn to a warrant charging her with attempted blackmail. The days passed. The case was not called.

Every day was an agony for Sally. The thought of the dying baby was like a hot coal on the girl's mind. She went to the matron about it. The matron went out to see the baby. When she returned she told Sally she had taken it to a hospital.

The Salvation Army used to visit the jail and get the prisoners to sing hymns. Sally joined in the chorus. A male prisoner heard her. He went out the next day for the Ohio pen to spend the rest of his life there. But he left a present for Sally with the desk sergeant. "Give these two bucks to the girl with the voice, will you?" he said. "Her singing did a lot for me."

Sally was finally called before the night court. The man did not appear. She was dismissed with a reprimand. As she passed the desk sergeant he handed her the two dollars. The gift finished the wreck of Sally's broken life.

She was in such a hurry to get out she ran down the halls, the matron rushing along at her side. "It's too bad, honey, they brought you in here. You didn't deserve it. I'm awful sorry for you." As Sally got to the door, she touched her elbow.

"Honey, I hate to tell you—the poor little baby is dead!"

It was like a ruffian blow struck across the **face**

of a little child. It stunned Sally—left her limp
and quivering. The baby was dead—

With a feeble, tormented sob, she put her hands
over her head and began to run as though men and
women were chasing her, pelting her with stones.

"Listen, honey," the matron caught up with her.
"You can stay here. It won't do you no good to get
out. The baby died three days ago. Stay here for
a while."

"Oh, God, no. Let me get out."

The door opened and the half-demented creature
ran out, one thought uppermost. She would go
down to the river. The blasting wind tore the clothes
almost off her back. The chill went to the marrow.

A light flared out from a shop window, the girl
dallied a moment in its warmth. Old jewelry, em-
blems, silver plate glinted in the show case. In one
corner were three revolvers. Sally looked at them
fascinated. A cold fury of revenge swept over her.

Up to that moment the anguish of loss ate at her—
she had seen only the suffering baby face. Now she
saw the man and the lashing contempt on his handsome features. She went in and bought one of the
pistols.

As soon as she had it in her hands, it seemed pulling her down like a coffin weight. She dropped it
in her blouse and went out, scooting down one street
and up another, so cold, so frenzied, so impatient for
the morning to come she did not even know that
she was crying and calling out in her misery until a
drunken old woman stopped her.

The bedraggled old creature took hold of her and

Sally let herself be jostled along to the dark, wretched hole where the woman lived. She lit a charcoal stove, and in its feeble glow Sally tried to warm herself.

The damp hole was alive with baleful shadows. Across the bare walls evil figures passed. Now it was the man as he stood rigid and beckoned to the police—now the hulking officer lurching forward, grabbing her by the shoulders. And again it was the mother and sisters, hunting the girl down with their scornful looks.

Only once did Sally see the baby. It seemed to be lying on the floor, its mouth writhing, its little hands opening and closing. The father walked up to it and brought his boot down on the plaintive little face, crushing the scalp and mangling the tender flesh.

"God, God, save!" Sally called out as the nightmare passed.

At last it was morning. Sally had to wait until noon. Not for one moment had her resolution faltered. She went straight to the bank and stood behind a column waiting for the man. It seemed that every one in the building rushed out at the stroke of 12—every one but Philip Austin.

Sally began to tremble. She put her hand to her pocket. The pistol was there. "Send him out quick, quick," she chattered in an insane prayer. "Send him out before I lose courage."

Down the street came a policeman. Sally cowered behind the stone pillar. The officer eyed her, walked a few paces, looked back and went on.

"Nobody here now, nobody here," Sally muttered to herself. "Send him out now."

A big form strode down the corridor and the next second Philip Austin swung through the door. Proud and magnificent, he walked like a prince. He walked as he did that joyous day when he swept his hat down in a lordly salute as Sally came down the cathedral steps. He had the same kingly smile on his lips.

Sally's nerve went loose as a taut string when one end is suddenly released. She ran up to him piti-ful, distracted, beside herself with misery.

"Phil—oh, Phil, the baby died! You put me in jail—and it died. It died without any one near it. It died because you wouldn't take care of it."

Not knowing what she was doing or saying in her beating grief, Sally flung herself into Austin's arms.

"The baby died—it's dead, dead. Oh, Phil, the baby is dead!"

With one swift, angry wrench the man caught her violently by the wrists.

"———— ———— you, you little hag—what do I care about your brat! Let it die. Now go—and don't hang around slopping tears at me. Let the brat die!"

Cold, scornful contempt scowling his features, Austin went to shove Sally from him. There was a little gasp, a tussle, a scream of hurt, sobbing agony, and the double-action revolver was jammed against the man's stomach.

"You don't care? Oh, God!" The trigger snapped.

"He looked me straight in the eye. He looked startled and frightened. He knew I did it. I saw it in his eye. He looked at me for just a moment and then he went down in a slump as though his backbone had suddenly melted."

From everywhere men and women darted into the street. They leaned over the prostrate form. And when they saw that the banker's son was dead, they turned on Sally with their fists and one giant tore her cheek open with a vicious blow.

"But he knew I did it. I saw that in his last glance!" Sally's face was daubed with tears, but there was a triumphant smile in her eye at the memory of Austin's death. "That's satisfaction enough for me. I'm content to spend my days here."

The girl's trial had taken just one day. The jury found her guilty. She was nineteen. That fact saved her from the death penalty.

Sally was a Southerner, with all the hot, proud vengeance of Kentucky in her veins. Her story moved me more than all the horrors I had felt in prison. I could understand the murderous fury that swept over her when the fellow turned her down. I went to the warden's office and blurted the whole story out to him.

"When I hear things like this, I want to leave the damn' hell." Darby did resign eventually because he could not endure the job of electrocuting the condemned. "But some one's got to be here. I hope I do the service well."

Darby said he would try for a pardon. It would have been granted on his recommendation, but the family of the dead man heard about it. They weren't satisfied with the mischief their blackguard son had already done. They went to work and villified Sally until there wasn't a scrap of flesh left on her bones. The pardon was denied.

Every time I heard that voice with its cascade of golden notes rippling down from the convict women's loft in the chapel it sent daggers through me.

This was a tale, it seemed to me, worthy of the genius of Bill Porter. I told it to him the next afternoon. He listened rather indifferently and when I was finished, he turned to Billy Raidler, "I've brought you a box of cigars."

I was furious at his unmoved coldness. I turned my back on him in angry humiliation. I wanted Porter to write a story about Sally—to make the world ring with indignation over the wrong that had been done. And the story did not seem to make the slightest impression on him. At that time my taste ran entirely to the melodrama. I could not understand Porter's saner discrimination.

He had distinct theories as to the purpose of the short story. We often discussed it. Now it seemed to me that he was deliberately refusing to carry out his ideas.

"The short story," he used to say, "is a potent medium of education. It should combine humor and pathos. It should break down prejudice with understanding. I propose to send the down-and-outers into the drawing-rooms of the 'get-it-alls,' and I intend to insure their welcome. All that the world needs is a little more sympathy. I'm going to make the American Four Hundred step into the shoes of the Four Million."

Porter said this long before any of the stories that make up "The Four Million" had been written.

"Don't you think Sally's story has the real heart throb in it?"

"Colonel, the pulse beats too loud," Porter yawned. "It's very commonplace."

"And so is all life commonplace," I fired back. "That's just what genius is for—you're supposed to take the mean and the ordinary and tell it in a vital way—in a way that makes the old drab flesh of us glow with a new light."

I also was writing a story in those days and I had my own methods and theories. They usually dried out when I tried to run them into the ink well and onto the paper.

There was no use in trying to coax Porter into conversation when he was not in the mood. If a thing didn't catch his interest at once, it never did. There were no trials over with him. The slightest detail would sometimes absorb him and seem to fill him with inspiration. And again, a drama would pass before him and he would let it go unmarked. I knew this. I had seen him coolly ignore Louisa and old man Carnot often enough. But I was just goaded into persistence.

"Sally has a face like Diana," I said.

"When did you meet the goddess, colonel?" Porter jested, all at once absorbed in flicking a bit of dust from his sleeve. "Convict wool is shoddy enough, let alone a convict bundle of muslin."

A few years later. I saw this very same man go into all the honkatonks of New York and no woman

was too low to win courtesy from Bill Porter. I
have seen him treat the veriest old hag with the
chivalry due a queen.

His indifference to Sally's plight was singular.
If he had seen her and talked to her I know it would
have gripped him to the heart.

Porter saw that I was bitterly wounded and in the
petting kind of a way he had he came over to win
me back.

"Colonel, please don't be angry with me. You
misunderstand me. I wasn't thinking much of Sally
tonight. My mind was far away," he laughed. "It
was down in Mexico, perhaps, where that indolent,
luxurious valley of yours is and where we might
have been happy.

"Colonel," Porter's face lighted with humorous
eagerness, "do you think we stand any chance to collect that $7,000 you paid down on it? I'm a little in
need of funds."

Not many could resist the winning magnetism of
Bill Porter if he chose to make himself agreeable.
As soon as he had spoken I knew that some secret
grief was tugging at him. Porter had labored hard
over some story—Billy Raidler had sent it out in the
usual way for him. It had come back. He jested
about it.

"The average editor," he said, "never knows a fire-
cracker until he hears the bang of its explosion.
Those fellows can't tell a story until some one else
takes the risk of setting it off."

"They're a damn' bunch of ignoramuses!" Porter
had read the story to Billy and me and we had sent it

off with singing hearts. We were sure the world must acknowledge Porter, even as we did.

"All I'm sorry for is the loss of the stamps Billy was forced to steal from the State to mail it with. It may damage the reputation of the State board of the Ohio penitentiary," Porter replied, but he was really disappointed. The rejection of his manuscripts did not dull the edge of his self-confidence, but filled him with forebodings as to his future.

"I should not like to be a beggar, colonel," he often said, "and my pen is the only investment I can make. I am continually paying assessments on it. I would like to collect a few dividends."

That same story paid its dividends later. Porter revamped it here and there and it made a big hit for him.

"I'll tell you why I'm not interested in Sally," he swung back to the subject with a suddenness that startled me. "She's better off here than she ever could be outside. I know this place is doom—but what chance has a girl with Sally's past in the world? What are you thinking of, colonel, when you plan to send the girl out there to be trampled in the gutter?"

Sally said almost the same words to me when I tried to get her a pardon after I was freed. I went back to the pen to see her.

"Oh, Mr. Jennings!" Her face had grown thin and its transparent whiteness made her seem a thing of unearthly spirituality. "Don't bother about me. I'm lost. You know it. Do you think they would ever let me crawl back? You know I'm a bad woman.

"I had a baby that I didn't have any right to—do you think the world ever forgives such a crime as that? Leave me alone here. I'm finished. There's no pardon on earth for me."

CHAPTER XXII.

Sally was right. There was no place for her in the outside world. The ex-convict is thrown against a social and economic boycott that no courage or persistence can effectively break.

We talked about it often—Bill Porter and I. It was the topic of eternal interest just as the discussion of dress is with women. And yet, for Porter, this talk about the future was an unalloyed torment. It agitated and distressed him. He would come into the post-office of an evening and we would gossip with fluent merriment. Without prelude, one of us would mention a con who had been sent back on another jolt. All the whimsical light that usually played about his large, handsome face would give place to a shadow of heavy gloom. The quick, facile tongue would halt its whispering banter.

Bill Porter, the wag, became Bill Porter, the cynic. Fear of the future was like a poisonous serpent that had coiled into his heart and lodged there, its fangs striking into the core of his happiness.

"The prison label is worse than the brand of Cain," he said many a time. "If the world once sees it, you are doomed. It shall not see it on me. I will not become an outcast.

"The man who tries to hurl himself against the tide of humanity is sure to be sucked down in the undertow. I am going to swim with the current."

Porter had less than a year more to serve. He was already planning on his re-entrance to the free world. For me the question did not then exist. My sentence was life. But I felt that Porter's position was false. I knew that it would mean an unsheathed sword perpetually hanging over his head. The fear of exposure saddened and almost tragically hounded his life.

"When I get out, I will bury the name of Bill Porter in the depths of oblivion. No one shall know that the Ohio penitentiary ever furnished me with board and bread.

"I will not and I could not endure the slanting, doubtful scrutiny of ignorant human dogs!"

Porter was an enigma to me in those days. There was no accounting for his moods. He was the kindest and most tolerant of men and yet he would sometimes launch into invective against humanity that seemed to come from a heart charged with contemptuous anger for his fellows. I learned to understand him later. He liked men; he loathed their shams.

The freemasonry of honest worth was the only carte blanche to his friendship. Porter would pick his companions from the slums as readily as from the drawing-rooms. He was an aristocrat in his culture and his temperament, but it was an aristocracy that paid no tribute to the material credentials of society.

Money, fine clothes, pose—they could not hoodwink him. He could not abide snobbery or insincerity. He wanted to meet men and to make friends with them—not with their clothes and their bank accounts. He knew an equal even when hidden in rags—and he could scent an inferior underneath a wealth of purple and fine linen.

Porter dealt with the fundamentals in his human relations. He went down under the skin. And so he scoffed at conventional standards of appraising men and women. He belittled the paltry claims whereon the shallow minded based their supposed prestige.

"Colonel," he would mock, "I have a proud ancestry. It runs back thousands and thousands of years. Do you know, I can trace it clear back to Adam!

"The man I would like to meet is the one whose family tree does not take its root in the Garden of Eden. What an oddity he would have to be—a sort of spontaneous creation.

"And, colonel, if the first families only looked far enough back, they would find their poor, miserable progenitors blindly wallowing about in the slime of the sea!"

That any of these descendants of slime should dare to look down upon him even in thought was intolerable. He knew himself to be the equal of all men. His fierce, honest independence would brook patronage from none.

"I won't be under an obligation to any one. When I get out from here I'll strike free and bold. No one shall hold the club of ex-convict over me."

"Other men have said the same." I felt that Porter's attitude lacked courage. "And there is always some one to hunt them down. You can't get away with it."

"You can't beat the game if any one ever finds out you once were a number," Porter flung back, riled and indignant that he was forced to defend himself. "The only way to win is to conceal."

Every day incidents happened to bear out Porter's argument.

Men would be sent out and in a few months they were back. The past was their scourge. They could not escape its lash. And just a few weeks after we had talked about the thing—a few weeks after I had told him of Sally—Foley the Goat and the sinister tragedy that followed him threw us all into a hot fury of resentment and rage.

Foley's misfortune made a tremendous impression on Porter. The incident was directly responsible for the breakup of the Recluse Club.

After Porter was transferred to the steward's office, three weeks passed and he had not come to one of our Sunday dinners. His absense was as depressing as a cold rain on a May Day fête. The club was lifeless without him. Even Billy Raidler's bubbling raillery simmered down.

Old man Carnot grew more querrulous when his napkin was carelessly folded and Louisa could not argue the beginning and the end of Creation. When he started in to divide Infinity there was no one to oppose him.

I took Bill's absence as a personal insult. I felt that a friend had forgotten me.

We were sitting at the table on the fourth Sunday. We had a wretched meal. No one had been able to bring in the bacon.

I usually procured the roast. I would take over about two dollars in stamps to the guard at the commissary and this State official would open the door and allow me to take all that I could carry.

A new guard had come in. I was afraid to try the old tactics on him. Louisa had been equally unfortunate. We had nothing but some leftover potatoes, some canned string beans and stale doughnuts for the weekly feast.

"Where is Mr. Bill?" old Carnot complained. "Has the man's promotion inflated his self-esteem? By Jove, does he not realize that the name Carnot is one of the proudest in New Orleans!" He was sputtering and fuming.

"Mr. Carnot, a name may be your pass-key to the domains of the élite," I tried to taunt him. "But Bill Porter has an inner circle of his own. He doesn't care what your credentials are!"

I went over to the window and looked across the prison campus, hoping that Bill might be coming along. I was about to give up when I saw his portly figure swinging hurriedly but with calm dignity down the alley.

"Fellow comrades—the prodigal returns and he brings the fatted calf with him," Porter's full gray eyes gleamed, and he began to empty his pockets. A small dray could not have carried much more. There were French sardines, deviled ham, green peas, canned chicken, jellies and all manner of delicacies.

We looked on as Lazarus might have when an extra fat crumb fell from Dives' table.

It was a joyous reunion. It was the last meeting of the Recluse Club. A bitter feud grew up between its members. The case of Foley the Goat and Porter's indignant sympathy brought to its end the one pleasant feature of our prison life.

There are some men who are conquered only by death. They will not yield even though life is the penalty for rebellion. Men of this type can no more survive in prison than a free-thinking private can in the army.

They do not fit in with the crushing discipline of penitentiary life. They are marked for a quick finish the moment their heads are shaved and their chests hung with a number. The man who will not bend is broken. It is the inevitable law of prison life.

The prison guard will not endure defiance. It whips the beast in him to a frenzy. In the Ohio pen they had a way of eliminating the unruly. The trip-hammer at bolt contract was their neat manner of execution.

Foley the Goat was one of these incorrigibles. He was more hateful to the guards than leprosy. They sent him to the trip-hammer. The man consigned to that labor is doomed. There is no reprieve for him. He cannot endure the terrific grind more than three or four months—then he is carted to the hospital to rack out a few breaths before going to the trough.

Death was a 'mighty-severe sentence for Foley.

His capital sin was his fearless independence. He would fling back an angry retort to a guard even though he knew that the flesh would be stripped from his back in payment. He was consistent in his defiance. No one ever heard the Goat send up a yell from the basement. It gave him an odd reputation in the pen. To the other prisoners he seemed a man protected by a sort of witchcraft.

"He is possessed of the devil," they would whisper in awed admiration. "It ain't in flesh and blood to stand it. He's thrown a spell about himself. He don't feel!"

"Sure, he's in cohoots with the Old Fellow," another would volunteer. "He had ghosts rifling the purses of Columbus for him after he cleaned out all the pockets in Cincinnati."

The superstitious believed it, and if ever there was a man about whom the mantle of mystery draped itself with a natural grace it was Foley the Goat. He was almost unbelievably lean- and hollow-looking and his eye was the most compelling and fiery thing I had ever looked upon.

I never will forget the quivering throb of interest that caught me the first time I saw that smoldering red-brown eye flaming out its defi' at the prison guard.

I had stopped to give an order from the warden. A tall, angular, unsubstantial fellow came with nervous swiftness toward us. He moved with such rapidity he seemed to be winging across the grass. The breath of an instant that hurried figure paused in its ardent walk and the man lashed upon the guard the burning light of his scornful eye. It was uncanny. It went over the guard like a malignant curse.

"Damn' Beanpole!" The guard set his teeth. "He'll get his—damn his bewitched eye!"

"Who is it?"

"Who? Devil take him—the Goat, of course. He murders men with his looks. Who else would dare do it? He's got about three months more to live, damn him!"

Foley was the master pickpocket of Ohio. His nimble fingers, with their ghostly lightness, had gathered a fortune. A mean and paltry profession it seemed to me until I talked about it to Foley. He had as much pride in his "gift" as a musician, or a poet, or a train-robber has in his. But Foley's art was not in the accepted curriculum. He was sent up for two years.

They had been two years of relentless punishment for Foley. He was early initiated into the horrors of the basement. The man was neither desperate nor vicious but he did not know how to cringe when a guard demanded groveling obedience. Foley was an indomitable, angry sort. He could not be subdued and so he was all but murdered. He came into the pen weighing 200 pounds. When I saw him he carried but 142 pounds on his six-foot frame.

He had been two months at the trip-hammer when his term expired. In the bolt contracts this massive instrument was operated by man power. It was a cruel and driving job. For 60 days his arms and legs had been in almost perpetual motion. The big hammers were pedaled by the feet, small ones by the hand.   Sixty days had finished the wreck of Foley's constitution.

The end of his term saved him from death.

He was but a shadow when he came into the warden's office for his discharge.   "I'm finished with the game," there was no surrender in his intrepid red-brown eyes, though his voice was but a hoarse, shocking whisper and his hands were transparent.

"I'm done in," he said without a trace of self-pity or regret.   "I'm going to wind it up peacefully on the hill where I was born.   I've got a few thousand. That'll pay for a funeral.   I've had 28 years on this planet—that's   enough.   I'm   satisfied—my   last breath will be a free one!"

Foley reckoned without Cal Crim.   He reckoned without the boycott.   He forgot that he was ligitimate prey to be hunted down as soon as his release became known.

And so he went about his home city as though he were in truth a free man.   At the corner of Fifth and Vine streets he discovered his mistake.

Foley stood there one night, aimless enough to be sure.   It was but a week or so after his discharge. The ex-con was waiting for a little old lady.   He was going to take her to a vaudeville show.

The little old creature was his aunt.   She had raised him.   When he came out from the pen she took him back to the little house where he was born. Tonight they were going on a glorious lark.   She would be coming along in a few moments.   So Foley waited.

A man saw him standing there.   He watched and

after a while he slouched up from behind and caught
Foley by the arm.

"Hello, Goat, when did you get back?" Cal Crim,
a big rough-neck bull in the Cincinnati department,
leered at Foley.

"Hello, Cal," Foley was not suspicious. He had
kept his resolution. He had neither the wish nor the
need to steal. "I got back last week."

"Been to headquarters yet?" Crim tightened his
clutch on Foley's skeleton arm.

"Not much. I'm through. I've given up the old
game."

"Don't rib me, you damn' thief. I am a wise guy,
I am. Get along, you sneak," he had Foley by the
neck and was pushing him forward. "I'll take you
to headquarters?"

The Goat knew what that meant. He wouldn't
have a chance at that last free breath. Once at
headquarters and conviction was certain.

"Let go, you skunk, Crim, or I'll kill you!" Foley
wrenched himself free and turned on the cop. "Don't
bully me, Crim. You got nothin' on me. Drop your
damn' hands or I'll finish you."

Crim was a hulking giant. He swept out his club.

"Walk along, you thief, or I'll bring this down
on your lying head!"

Foley squirmed. There was a crack, a thud and
a livid welt with the blood bursting through stood out
on Foley's cheek. Crim yanked him to his feet.
Foley's terrible eyes glared at him. His lightning
fingers went to his pockets. An old .44 bulldog
pistol went against the bull's stomach. Five shots

and the fellow crumpled into a nerveless heap at Foley's feet.

There was no vaudeville that night for Foley the Goat and his little old aunt. He was nailed. They rustled him off to jail and booked him with "Assault with attempt to kill."

I don't know where the five shots went, but Cal Crim didn't die. I've hated a bulldog pistol ever since. At the hospital he came to and began screaming in a horrible frenzy—"There's Foley—that shadow—catch it—out with your club, quick—the damn' skeleton, he's so thin there's nothing left to beat."

No need to nail Foley. He was finished. He had gone out from the pen shrunken to bones—nothing but a hoarse choking cough. The cowardly blow that came smashing down on his face, knocking his rickety body to the ground, took out his last ounce of fight. The longest term the court could give Foley would be a light sentence.

When the news hit the pen that Foley was up for another jolt, hot suppressed anger, a thousand times more resentful because it had no outlet—the futile champing fury of chained beasts—went in a muttering bitterness from shop to shop.

Each convict saw in Foley an image of himself. His fate represented their future. They looked upon this fighting, unruly fellow as the devoted venerate, a martyr.

Men, who longed to "sass" the guards but lacked the nerve felt that Foley's reckless temerity redeemed their independence. He did what they dared only to imagine. Sometimes I would hear the men repeating one-sided insults from the guards.

"Damn' scoundrels—just wait till I get out of here. The bloodhounds, they'll whimper to my lash!"

Such dreams of vengeance as they cherished. How they would get even for all the raw indignities they had suffered! Like dogs they had fawned under the scourge. Some day they would be free! Foley's doom chilled the hope in every heart.

We took up a collection for the Goat. Not many of us had any spending money. Billy Raidler and I contributed 50 cents each in stamps. This was a small fortune in the prison. Except for men whose families kept them supplied, like Old Carnot and Louisa, very few of the prisoners had more than a few bits at a time.

Some gave a nickel, others a dime and some a penny. Every cent meant a sacrifice. Men went without pie or coffee at night to get their names down on Foley's subscription list.

Billy and I brought the paper over to Old Man Carnot. We expected a handsome donation from him—a dollar perhaps.

"My word, Billy, what nonsense is this!" The fringe of hair stuck out like a double row of red pins around his fat face and his pursy lips sputtered a shower at us. "Why, Foley is a common pickpocket! He should be in jail. It is most arrant foolishness to send a donation to the poor-white trash!"

"You white-livered old reprobate, if I had five fingers I'd tear the guts out of you!"

It was the first time I had ever seen Billy angry.

His long, slender body trembled; his face seemed suddenly blotched with rage and he leaned against me heavily.

"Damn you, Carnot, you better thank heaven I can't spring at you. If I could stand alone, you'd hit the hay and never wake up!"

"Is he serious, Mr. Jennings?" The old fool moved back in shocked astonishment. "Does he really wish the release of this villainous pickpocket?"

"Carnot, you're a lying hypocrite. We've got your number, all of us. You're a rotten embezzler and you stole $2,000,000. You're a blackguard and every cent you own is filthy with the tears and blood of white trash. You're a damn' skunk and we wouldn't let you give a cent to a real man!"

If Foley could have seen Carnot's distorted face he would have been compensated for the loss of the dollar. We went to Louisa. He was busy writing out specifications in the contract shop.

"I'm too busy—it doesn't interest me!"

That ended it. We didn't give Louisa another chance. Neither of us was in the mood for explanations.

"Put me down for a dollar! I'll raise my subscription. I've struck it rich."

We were in the post-office that evening. Billy's income had suddenly jumped. It was an unstable account. He kept the nail on his index finger long and sharp. He would whiffle it under the edge of uncancelled stamps that came on the mail to the post-office. Sometimes the revenue went to $5 or $6 a month.

The officials knew of all these practices of ours. They knew of the existence of the club, they knew of the little thefts whereby men gained enough to buy tobacco or candy. But they made no effort to remedy conditions. It would have been futile.

The evils were inherent in a system that compelled men to live starved and abnormal lives. There were so many graver crimes committed even by the officials themselves in order that the prison system be maintained.

Billy had neatly folded off seven stamps—one of them was worth 10 cents.

"Did you ever see such an ugly red sinner as old Carnot? I'd rather be lackey to a nigger than God to such a sputtering lobster. I'd be glad to roast in hell for the pleasure of seeing his fat self-satisfied hide on the grid."

"Hot satisfaction, indeed!" The door was shoved gently open and Porter's understanding eyes went in amusement over Billy's excited face.

"Who's damned now?" Profanity was not one of Porter's weaknesses. "It is a good vent for the ignorant. It is but a cheap outlet," he would rail at me when Billy and I would volley out a hot shot of "damns" and "by Gods."

"What joint is now out of socket in this Paradise of the Lost?"

We told him about the subscription for Foley the Goat and the refusal of Carnot and Louisa to subscribe.

"Pusillanimous, penurious pickpockets that they are—dastardly defaulters, who would expect largesse from them? It but increases my respect for bankers of your type, colonel."

Porter gave a dollar to the fund. He had sold some story—I do not remember the name, but I think it was "Christmas by Injunction."

"I would have expected better of Louisa." Porter had a deep affection for the clever, brilliant thinker. "I do not wish to see either of them again. This refusal to help Foley is too shoddy."

Money never meant anything to Porter—when he had it he spent it freely. He placed no value on it except the power it gave him to gratify the thousand odd impulses that were the very life of him.

When Louisa heard of Porter's indignation, he sent him a detailed explanation. There were at least 15 typewritten pages.

"I have another newspaper from Lizzie." He showed us the bulky manuscript. Louisa and Porter were given to correspondence. The ex-banker's letters were masterpieces. He discussed philosophy, science and art in a way that filled Porter with delight.

"I haven't had time to read it all, but he says he did not think. He did not give the matter of Foley a second thought. That's the trouble with the world —it doesn't think. But the fellow who is starving or trampled on is compelled to think. If men would investigate the claims of others and their justice, the human heart would beat with a kinder throb."

We did not go over to the club that Sunday. Louisa was broken-hearted. Old man Carnot raged and fumed. None of us ever bothered with him again. The happy association was ended. With its break, a deeper friendship between Porter and myself was cemented.

We got up $25 for Foley. I wrote a letter of appreciation extolling his valorous deed in attacking the cop. Porter leaned over my shoulder. "Be not so exuberant in your praise, colonel. They may come in here and get us and hold us 'particeps criminis after the act.' I should not like to be branded as a murderer and compelled to remain longer even in the company of such choice spirits as Billy and yourself."

"You're not exactly in your element here, are you, Bill?"

"As much at home and as comfortable as a fly in a spider's embrace."

"Do you think that society is any better off because a few thousand men are put behind bars?"

"If we could select the right 'few thousand,' society would benefit. If we could put in the real scoundrels, I would favor prisons. But we don't. The men who kill in legions and who steal in seven figures are too magnificent in their criminality to come under the paltry observance of law and order. But fellows like you—well, you deserved it all right."

Porter turned the argument off with a laugh. He was a good bit of a standpatter even after two years and three-quarters in the pen. He did not like to discuss prison affairs. His apathy nettled me so much that I could never overlook an opportunity to goad him.

"Money and lives are wasted. Just consider the energies that go to the devil in here. Under a better plan, prisoners could be punished without being damned."

"Colonel, you're fantastic. What sort of a fourth dimension jail would you suggest?"

"I would not throw men in a hog pen and expect them to come out cleaner than they went in. No state is rich enough to maintain a breeding place for crime and degeneracy. That's what a modern prison is.

"Men are cut off from their families; they are thrown into shameful and degrading cells, where the sanitary conditions would disgust a self-respecting pig; they are compelled to fawn to bullying guards—no wonder they come out more like animals than men. They are cut off from every decency and refinement of life and are expected to come back reformed."

"The world is very illogical," Porter tilted back on the high stool in the post-office, reached up to the desk for a magazine and started to read.

"When you get out you can bring the matter before the public. With your gift, you can do wonders to break down the system."

"I shall do nothing of the kind."

It was Bill's touchy spot. He snapped forward on the stool, dropping the magazine on the table.

"I shall never mention the name of prison. I shall never speak of crime and punishments. I tell you I will not attempt to bring a remedy to the diseased soul of society. I will forget that I ever breathed behind these walls."

I could not understand Porter on this score. I

knew that he was neither cold nor selfish, yet he seemed almost stoically unconcerned about the horrors that went on in prison. He could never bear to hear an allusion to Ira Maralatt. He did not want to meet Sally and he refused almost with violence to come into the chapel to hear her sing. Yet when the persecution of Foley ended in a sordid tragedy, he was swept into a scornful fury for the whole infamous system responsible for the rank outrage. It was a mystery to me.

CHAPTER XXIII.

O. Henry's rage against corruption; zeal yields to prudence; a draft of the grafter's wine.

"You're right. Prisons are a joke, but the grim laugh is on the fellow who gets caught." Bill Porter had pushed the door of the post-office open. No greeting; no amiable raillery; no droll quips. Abruptness was a new mood even with this whimsical chameleon.

"I'm on the edge of the abyss. I'm going to jump over."

I looked at him, amazed at the astounding confession. Something unusually shocking and sinister must have happened to throw Bill Porter's reticent, proud self-possession into open despondency. His face was drawn and worried, the usually quiet, appraising gray eyes were shot through with nervous anger and for once the silky yellow hair was frayed down over his forehead.

"Caged beasts are free compared to us. They aren't satisfied to stunt our bodies—they damn our souls. I'm going to get out."

Porter let himself slump down on the straightback chair and sat regarding me in silence.

"Al, I ran into a mess today so foul a leper would fight shy of it. And they want me to stick my hands into it! You were right. The crimes that men are paying for behind these walls are mere foibles compared to the monstrous corruption of the free men on the outside.

"Why, they walk into the State treasury and fill their pockets with the people's gold and walk out again and no one even mentions a word of the theft. And I'm supposed to put my signature to the infamous steal! Colonel, they'd make you look like a pickpocket—the colossal thievery they're going to put over!"

"Whose dopin' out the medicine, Bill? When do they tackle the job? I might hold the horses, you know, and collect my divvy." Porter tossed his head in irritable impatience. "This is tragic. Don't be the jester at a funeral. You know that requisition for meat and beans you sent over? Do you know what happened and what is about to happen?"

I had a pretty good idea. I had been "wised up" to the practice. As secretary to the warden I gave the order for all purchases required in the penitentiary. If the State shop wanted wool, or the bolt contract needed steel or the butcher shop meat, the lists were sent into the warden's office. I sent the requisitions to the steward and Bill Porter, as his secretary, was supposed to let out the bids. The merchant on the outside would then contract to keep us supplied for a specified length of time.

There were certain big business men who solicited the prison trade. When the bids were called for, these men would send in prices far in excess of the market values. The bids were, of course, supposed to be secret and the lowest man was presumably given the deal. In practice, however, the letting of the bids was an empty formality.

The state and prison officials had friends. The bids would be opened and if the friend had not guessed right, he would be tipped off and allowed to submit another bid just a fraction less than the lowest. He would then send to the pen the most inferior products, charging an incredibly exorbitant price.

The State paid enough to run the prison as a first-class hotel. The food it received was so wretched it broke down the health and ruined the digestion of the most robust. It was the same with every other commodity purchased for prison use.

"Do you know what happened?" Porter repeated. There was a grating harshness in the low voice. "The bids came in today. The prices were outrageous. I had made a study of the market values. I wished to refer the bids back to the contractors and demand a fair rate. The suggestion was ignored.

"That was not the worst of it. The contract was not given to the lowest bidder, but to another. He was informed of his competitor's figure and allowed to underbid it by one cent. It means that the taxpayers of this community are deliberately robbed of thousands and thousands of dollars on this one contract alone. And a convict who is here on a charge of taking a paltry $5,000, not one cent of which he ever got, must be a party to the scandal."

"You know of these things, Al?" It seemed to prick Porter that I was not greatly impressed.

"Sure, Bill. Here, take a gulp for your misery." I poured him a glass of fine old burgundy. "Pretty good, isn't it? It came from the fellow who got the last bean contract. My predecessor left it here for me. Like as not we'll be in line now for all manner of presents from the thieves whose purses we help to line."

Porter pushed the wine from him. "Do you mean to say, Al, that you will wink at such outrageous crime? Why, the convicts doing life here are stainless compared to these highwaymen."

"Bill, you're up against it. You might as well be graceful about it. It would be easier for you to tear down these stone walls with your naked hand than to overthrow the iron masonry of political corruption. What can your protest accomplish? The system of legitimate stealing from the government was here long before we arrived. It will survive our puny opposition."

"I should prefer then to leave the steward's office. I shall hand in my resignation tomorrow." Porter got up to leave. He was just rash and impulsive enough to do the mad thing. I knew where he would end if he did. I didn't like the vision of the well-groomed and immaculate Bill heaped into a loathsome cell in solitary. Still less did I like the thought of him strapped over the trough and beaten to insensibility.

"Sit down, Bill, you damn' fool, and listen to reason." I caught his arm and pulled him back. "The government knows these criminals are at large. It likes them. It gives them wealth and homage. They're the big fellows of the State. They speak at all public meetings. They're the pillars of society."

Porter looked at me with an expression of repulsion.

"What do you propose to do about it?" I asked.

"I shall go to the officials of this institution. I will tell them I am not a thief, though I am a convict. I will defy them to sign up these infamous contracts. I will tell them to get another secretary."

"And the next day you will find yourself back in a mean little cell and in a week or so you'll be in solitary on a trumped up charge. And then you'll be torn up like Ira Maralatt. That's just about what your foolhardy honor will bring you."

A shadow went like a dark red scale over Bill's handsome face. He drew in his lips in disgust.

"By God, that would finish me."

He stood up, the panther in him ready to spring, just as it had leaped once before at the throat of the Spanish don. He flung out his hands as though he had suddenly found himself covered with odious welts from a guard's blows. "I'd wring their damn necks dry. Let anyone use me so!"

"You're nobody in particular except to yourself. You might as well look out for that self. Your whole future is absolutely ruined if you protest. The men you would balk are the biggest bugs in the country. They'd grind you right down to the dirt."

Porter sat there as though a sudden chill silence had frozen speech in him forever. The nine o'clock gong sounded. It was the signal for lights out. He started nervously toward the door and then came back, laughing bitterly.

"I thought I would get locked out. But I have a midnight key to the steward's office."

"Locked out? No such luck, Bill, we're just locked in."

He nodded. "Body and soul." He took up the glass of the grafter's wine, held it a moment to the light and with one gulp tossed it off.

It was the end of the struggle. The pulsing, clamorous silence that holds the tongue while thoughts shout from mind to mind was between us. Porter seemed exhausted by the defeat. The joy in his promotion was dissipated. He became more aloof than ever.

"What a terrible isolation there is in the prison life," he said after a pause that weighed like a stone upon us. "We are forgotten by the friends we left in the world and we are used by the friends we claim here."

I knew that Porter had a wife and child. I did not know then that he had reached his home after our separation in Texas to find his wife dying. Nor did I know that the $3,000 had given him a measure of independence in those last sad months before his trial and conviction.

In all our intimacy at prison, Porter never once alluded to his family affairs. Not once did he speak of the child who was ever in his thoughts. Billy and I sent out innumerable letters to little Margaret. Only once did Porter slip a word. It was that time when a story had been refused. He was disappointed, he said, for he had wanted to send a present to a little friend.

"We may not be forgotten by the folks on the outside," I offered.

"Forgotten or despised, what difference does it make? I left many there. They were powerful. They could have won a pardon for me." He looked at me with troubled suspense. "Al, do you think I am guilty?"

"No. Bill, I'd bank on you any day."

"Thanks. I've got one friend anyway. I'm glad they let me alone. I do not wish to be indebted to anyone. I am the master of my own fate. If I bungled my course and got myself here, then all right. When I get out I will be under an obligation to none."

Many of those friends would today hold it their highest honor to have aided O. Henry when he was just Bill Porter the convict. If anyone ever interested himself in Bill, he did not seem to know anything of it.

"I haven't much longer to stay here, colonel—how many contracts do you suppose there'll be to give out?"

"Oh, quite a few. Why?"

"There might be some way of escape for us."

"Yes, your way out is to feather your own nest and keep your trap shut. Take another swig."

After that there were many glasses of wine—many fingers of whiskey—many long conversations after the nine o'clock lights were out. Porter gave in, vanquished, but the surrender nagged at him like an ugly worm biting incessantly at his heart. He tried to keep the bids secret; he fought to give the contract to the lowest man. He would be asked to show the bids. He was a mere piece of furniture in the office. He had to do as he was told and without question.

"The dirty scoundrels," he would say to me.

"Pay no attention to it," I would advise. "Honesty is not the best policy in prison. Don't let it worry you."

"Of course I will not worry over it. We are nothing but slaves to their roguery."

Even so, Porter and I had tremendous power in letting out the contracts. The wealthy thieves, who profited at the expense of the State and two helpless convicts, sent us cases of the choicest wines. They sent us cigars and canned delicacies, as tokens of their esteem. We kept the contraband in the post-office and many a stolen feast, Billy and Porter and I enjoyed.

CHAPTER XXIV.

Tainted meat; O. Henry's morbid curiosity; his interview with the Kid
on the eve of execution; the Kid's story; the death scene;
innocence of the Kid.

I had nothing to do with the letting of the contracts, but the acceptance of the supplies was within the province of the warden's office. I knew the horrible starvation forced on the men in the main dining-room. The memory of my first meal there with the maggots floating in the stew gravy and the flies drowned in the molasses filled me with nausea every time I passed the kitchen.

I made up my mind for one thing . . . if towering prices were paid for meat, I would at least insist that the supply brought to the prison be wholesome.

"You can do that," Porter said. "The warden will bear you out on it. We can have that much satisfaction anyway."

When the first consignment came under the new contract, I went down to look at it. Prepared as I was for cheap substitutes, I was not ready for the shocking spectacle before me as the rotten stuff was shouldered out of the wagon.

"Put it back," I yelled. Breathless and fighting mad I reached the warden's office.

"They're unloading a lot of stinking, tainted meat down at the butcher shop. Flies wouldn't crawl in it, it's so rotten. It's an outrage. We've paid for prime roast beef. We've given the highest price ever quoted on the face of the earth for meat and they've brought us in a load of carrion. What shall I do about it?"

The warden turned a white, startled face toward me.

"What's this, what's this?" His voice sounded seared and faint to me. He started pacing the floor.

"It's a shame warden, the men are being starved. The beans are so old and withered and only famished men would besmirch themselves with that meat. We could at least require common wholesomeness."

"That's right, yes, that's right. You say the meat is absolutely tainted? Send it back. Write to them and tell them we demand good fare."

I made the letter strong enough to ring true. I informed the wholesalers that the Ohio penitentiary paid first-class prices. It demanded first-class produce. The meat we got after that was coarse, but it was fresh and clean.

I used this one authorization from the warden again and again to send back stuff. The contractors came to realize that the prison was no longer a garbage can for their spoiled supplies. They found it cheaper to send in a medium grade in the beginning.

"You've come to see there are worse things in the world, Bill, than an ex-convict," I suggested to Porter when I told him about the tainted meat. "When you get out will you brazen out their prejudice or will you keep to your old resolution?"

Porter had about four months more to serve. We

kept a calendar and every night we would strike off another day. It is a melancholy thing to feel the separation coming daily nearer—a separation that will be as final and uncompromising as death. We talked indifferently, almost flippantly at this time because we were so deeply touched.

"I have not changed. I will keep my word. What would you do, colonel, if you should get out?"

"I will walk up to the first man I see on the street and I will say to him. 'I'm an ex-con—just got out of the pen. If you don't like it, go to hell." (I did that very thing some years later.)

Porter burst out laughing. It was the first time I had ever heard him laugh outright. It seemed to come bubbling and singing up from his throat like a rich, sonorous tune.

"I would give a great deal for your arrogant independence. I wonder if I will regret my plan?"

I don't believe he ever did, even on the black day in New York when he all but admitted he could endure the suspense no longer.

"Is the fear of life greater than the fear of death, Al? Here I am ready to leave this pen and I am beset with anxieties lest the world may guess my past."

Porter didn't expect any answer to his question. He was in a sort of ruminating mood, liking to speak his thoughts aloud.

"How hard we work to make a mask to hide the real self from our fellows. You know I sometimes think the world would go forward at a lightning pace if men would meet each other as they are—if they could, even for a short time, put aside pose and hypocrisy.

"Colonel, the wiseacres pray to see themselves as others see them. I would pray rather that others might see us as we see ourselves. How much of hatred and contempt would melt in that clear stream of understanding. We could be equal to life if we tried hard enough. Do you think we could ever look into the face of death without a tremor?"

"I have seen men take a bullet and laugh with their last gasp. I have hidden out with the gang and every hide of us knew we were probably on our last stretch. None of us were squeamish about it."

"But there was uncertainty to give you hope. I am thinking of death that is as certain, say, as my release. Take, for instance, a condemned man—you know they are lashed with hideous nightmares. You have seen some of them die. Did any go fearlessly?

"I don't mean gameness or bravado, but downright absence of alarm. Did any one of them seem to grin in the teeth of death as though they were about to enter upon a sort of adventure?"

"Bill, you speak now of the fellows who pay for the drinks at their own funeral. The jailbird ain't that kind of an animal."

"I would like to talk to a man who looked at death. I would like to know what his sensations might be.

"I wonder if that's the reason Christ called Lazarus back—sort of wanted to know what the big jump might be like?"

It occurred to me that Porter was writing a story and wanted to daub the color on true. He never stuck to facts, but he went to no end of pains to set up his scenery aright.

"I can't produce a Lazarus to gratify your curiosity, but there's a fellow due to be bumped off in a week or so. You come over tomorrow and I'll knock you down to the nearstiff."

"What is he like?" Bill seemed all of a sudden to weaken and his fluent whispering became hesitant and uncertain.

"Don't know. But he'll sit in the chair in about ten days. He sent another fellow over the great divide some months ago. He says it's a lie and he's innocent just like a babe, you know."

There's nothing very esthetic in the prison soul. Men laugh and jest over death. For weeks we would know when the electric chair was due for a sitting. We would watch the condemned man walking in the yard with a special guard before he was finally locked up in the death cell and fattened for the slaughter.

"I'd change places, —— —— them, I'd die for the pleasure of gorging myself with a week of square meals." Many a time I have heard raw-boned, hungry-eyed men in the ranges and shops fling out the challenge.

But as the day for the official murder draws near, the whole place seems overhung with mournful gray shadows. One can almost feel it in the corridors— the cold, clammy atmosphere of the death-day. It is as though drowned people with wet hair clinging about their dead faces went drooping up and down reaching out chilly fingers and putting their icy touch on each man's heart.

We never talked on those days but often in the night, screams, long, frightful and sobbing—screams that trailed into broken agonized moans would split the air waking us with creeping foreboding. Some overwrought wretch whose dream tormented him had seen the death in his sleep.

There was that grewsome hubbub about the prison now for the Kid was going to be bumped off. They were extra busy in the electrical department—it takes plenty of juice to kill the condemned.

Porter came over to the campus to talk to the man who faced death. "There he is, the soft-looking fellow walking with the guard—he'll let you talk to him."

When a man has but seven or eight days of life they give him a few privileges even in a prison. They let him take a turn in the yard—they give him roast beef and chicken to eat. They let him read and write, and sometimes they let him keep his light all night. Darkness is such a dread magnifier of terrors.

Porter went over to talk to the Kid. The three men fell in together and walked up and down for about five or ten minutes. The condemned man put a hand on Bill's arm and seemed childishly pleased to have such company.

When Porter came back to me, his face was a sickish yellow and his short, plump hands were closed so tight the nails gored his flesh. He rushed into the post-office, sat down on a chair and wiped his face. The sweat stood out like heavy white pearls.

"Guess you got the scare, all right, Bill? Get a close enough squint at the old Scythe Dancer?" He looked as though he might have seen an unholy ghost.

"Al, go out and talk to the boy. Be quick. This is too monstrous. I thought he was a man. He is but a child. He has no fear. He can't seem to realize that they mean to kill him. He hasn't looked at death. He's too young. Something should be done about it."

I had not talked to the fellow. I knew he was up for murder. I thought he was about 25.

"Colonel, did you see the way he put his hand on my arm? Why he's only a little, ignorant fellow— he's just 17. He says he didn't do it. He's sure something will happen to save him.

"Good God, colonel, can a man believe any good of the world when cold-blooded murders like this are deliberately perpetrated? The lad may be innocent. Al—he has gentle, blue eyes—I've seen eyes like them in a little friend of mine. It's a damn' shame to murder him."

As the warden's secretary I had to attend and make a record of the executions. A soft youngster of 17 would make an ugly job for me.

I knew the facts in this case. The evidence was strong against the Kid. He and a boy friend had gone down to the Scioto river one Sunday afternoon to take a swim.

The Kid came back alone—the other boy was missing. Three weeks later a body was found in the mud far down the river. It was decomposed beyond the possibility of recognition. The face had been eaten away.

The parents of the missing boy had been haunting the morgue. They looked at the remains, found a birthmark on the decomposed body and established the identity of their son. The Kid was arrested. Witnesses clamored into the courtroom. They had seen two boys on the Scioto and the Kid was pointed out as one of them.

The boys had been quarreling. Suddenly the Kid had grabbed his companion by the arm, dragged him down to the river, shouting: "I'll drown you for this!" Two men and a woman had heard the threat. The Kid was condemned on their circumstantial evidence.

"Yes, sir, that's true." The youngster looked at me with his gentle eyes and put his hand on my arm as he had on Porter's.

"Thet's true, all right—but thet ain't all."

The Kid kept his hold on me as though he feared I might leave before he had a chance to speak. It was pathetic—his eagerness for company. We walked up and down in the sun and he looked at the sky and at the top of a tree whose branches reached over the wall. He said he wasn't afraid and there was no resentment in his expression—just gratitude for the pleasure of talking, it seemed.

"Yer see, Mr. Al, me and Bob Whitney went down to the river thet Sunday and we got to foolin' and wrestlin' 'round there and we wasn't mad et all, but maybe we looked like we was. He throwed me down and landed on top er me and I jumped up and yells that to him.

"I sed, 'I'll drown yer for this,' and I pulled him up and we bumped each other down to the water.

They was people there and they heard it, but we was only foolin'.

"I had to git back to work and I left Bob there and I never seed him again. And after a while thet body was washed up and they sed it was Bob and thet I drowned him and they tuk me into court and I got all twisted up.

"I told them it was all jest funnin' and I sed Bob was swimmin' 'round when I left, but they looked at me like I was lyin' and the judge sed, 'I sentence yer to die or somethin' like thet—

"But death don't skeer me—"

All the time he talked the Kid kept his rough, freckled hand on my arm. It sent a chill, creepy sensation up to my shoulder and across my neck. I never saw softer, kinder eyes than those that ignorant, undeveloped boy of 17 turned so persistently at me. The more he talked the harder it became to picture him walking to the electric chair.

I felt weak and sick at the thought of taking notes on this Kid's death agony. The sun was warm and gentle that day, and the Kid stood there as if he liked it and he kept looking up at the tree and then at me. He had such a boyish jaw and chin and a kind of likable pug nose that had nothing malicious about it— he didn't look like a murderer.

I could hardly imagine him capable even of anger. He seemed to grow younger with almost every sentence he uttered.

"Jest look et thet tree—ain't it a shinnin', though? We had a tree like thet in our back yard once when I was a kid. I ain't gonna show no yeller streak.

I ain't skeered to die. When I was a kid I had a li'l sister. I sold newspapers and uster come in late. We was all alone 'ceptin' for a old stepmother.

"Li'l Emmy uster creep up ter me and say, 'Aintcha skeered, Jim, to be out so late? Didjer bring me a cookie?' We uster have fine times eaten' the cakes.

"Then li'l Emmy got sick and the old hag—that's all we ever called her—beat her, and I got mad and we sneaked away and lived in a basement, and we was awful happy, 'cept thet li'l Emmy was skeered of everything.

"She was a-skeered to go out, a-skeered to stay home and she uster foller me 'round while I sold the papers. 'Bout 10 o'clock we'd go home. She'd hug on to my arm and whisper: 'You ain't skeered o' nuthin, are yer, Jim?' We treated ourselves to cookies and Emmy made coffee and we did jest whatever we wanted to.

"Then Emmy got sick agin and she died. She had li'l white hands, and one finger got chopped off'n her right hand when she was a baby. And the last thing she did 'fore she died—she put out her hands to me and she sed:

" 'Jim, you ain't skeered o' nuthin', are you? You ain't skeered to die?'

"And I ain't. I'm gonna walk right up ter thet chair same's it was a plush sofa 'fore a big fire."

It was an obsession with him.

"I've got a pass for you to see the Kid die," I said to Porter the night before the execution.

He looked at me as though I were a cannibal in-

viting him to partake of the flesh of some human
baby. He started up as though jerked by an electric
shock.

"Is that going through? My God, what a den of
depraved fiends this prison is! I'd rather see the only
thing I have on this earth dead at my feet than watch
the deliberate killing of the poor 'softy.' Excuse me,
colonel." Porter took up his hat and walked out of
the post-office. "I want to live a few weeks after I get
out of here."

I would like to have changed places with Bill.
Death hadn't any terrors for me—the elaborate ceremony they made of their murders. But I had to be
in the death cell when the kid was bumped off. He
came in between two guards. The chaplain walked
behind him, reading in a chanting rumble from an
open Bible. The Kid lopped in as though he had lost
control of his muscles; he appeared so loose limbed
and soft, and his pug nose stuck up, it seemed, more
than ever.

His gentle eyes were wide-open, glazed and terror-
stricken. His boyish face was ashen and his chin
shook so, I could hear his teeth knocking together.
The guard poured out a big glass of whiskey and
handed it to him.

It was a little custom they had to brace a man for
the last jolt.

The Kid pushed the glass from him, spilling the
liquor on the floor. He shook his head, his chin sagging
down and quivering.

"I don't need nutin', thanks." His face was bloodless as flour, and the frightened eyes darted from the

chair to the warden. He caught sight of me. I never felt so like a beast—so like an actor at a foul orgy—in all my life.

"Oh, Mr. Al—good mornin', mornin'." His head kept bobbing at me, so that I could see the big round spot on the crown where they had shaved the hair clean. One of the electrodes would be fastened on that shiny patch.

"Mornin', Mr. Al, I ain't skeered—what'd I tell you? I ain't skeered o' nuthin'."

The Kid's suit had been slit up the back seam so that the voltage could be shot through his body. He was led up to the chair, his shoulders and his elbows tied to its arms and the straps adjusted. The electrodes were placed against the bare calves of his legs and at the base of his brain.

It didn't take very long to make the complete adjustment, but to me it seemed that the ignoble affair would never be done with. When he was finally strapped down, the boy seemed about to collapse as though his bones had suddenly become jelly, but he was compelled to sit upright.

Warden Darby stepped up to the boy and called him by name.

"Confess, Kid," the warden's breath chugged out like a laboring engine's. "Just admit what you did and I'll save you. I'll get you a pardon."

The Kid sat staring at him and muttering to himself, "I ain't skeered, I tell yer."

"Confess, Kid," Darby yelled at him, "and I'll let you out."

The Kid heard at last. He tried to answer. His

lips moved, but none of us could hear his words. At last the sound came:

"I ain't guilty. I never killed him."

The warden threw on the lever. A blue flame darted about the Kid's face, singeing his hair and making the features stand out as though framed in lightning. The tremendous voltage threw the body into contortions, just as a piece of barbed wire vibrates out when it is suddenly cut from a fence. As the current went through him there came a little squeak from his lips. The lever was thrown off. The Kid was dead.

For a long time that night neither Porter nor I said a word. The whole prison seemed to be pressed down with an abject and sodden misery. The cons missed the Kid from the patch of sunlight in the yard. They knew he had been bumped off.

"Colonel, have you any special hope as regards heaven?" Porter had a glass of Tipo half raised to his lips. The grafters had sent us a new case of costly wines.

"Give me a swallow of that, Bill! it must have a wonderful kick in it—up to heaven in two gulps!" Porter ignored me. It was not a night for jest.

"I am not speaking of a churchly paradise, but what, Al, is your idea of a state of perfect bliss?"

"At present, Bill, a dugout way off in the wilderness, where I would never again see the faces of men. I would want plenty of cattle and horses, but no trace of the human kind except perhaps a few of their books."

"No, the books would spoil it. Don't you realize, colonel, that the serpent who wrecked the first para-

dise was Thought? Adam and Eve and all their unfortunate descendants might still be lolling in joyous
ignorance on the banks of the Euphrates if Eve hadn't
been stung with the desire to know. It's quite a
feather in a woman's cap. Mother Eve was the first
rebel—the first thinker."

Porter seemed impressed with his own brilliance.
He nodded his head to emphasize his conviction.
"Yes, colonel," he continued, "thought is the great
curse. Often when I was out on the Texas ranges I
envied the sheep grazing on the mesa. They are superior to men. They have no meditations, no regrets,
no memories."

"You're wrong, Bill, the sheep are more intelligent
than men. They mind their own business. They do
not take upon themselves the powers which belong
to Nature, or Providence, or whatever you wish to
call it."

"That's exactly what I finished saying. They do
not think; therefore they are happy."

"How stupid you are tonight, Bill. You might just
as well go into ecstasy over the joys of non-existence.
If thought makes us wretched, it is also thought that
gives us our highest delight."

"Certainly, if I did not think, I would be serenely
contented tonight. I should not be dragged down
with a ton weight of futile anger."

"And if you did not think, you would likewise be
incapable of intense pleasures."

"I have yet to find in thought, Al, this beneficent
aspect. I persist—Thought is a curse. It is responsible for all the viciousness found in the human family;

for depravities that are the monopoly of the lofty human species.

"Colonel—the Kid's execution is but one example of the viciousness of Thought. Men think a thing is and they conclude that it must be so. It is a sort of hypnotism."

Porter was never yet coherent in his philosophical pickings. He would begin with a whimsical absurdity and he would use this as a kind of string for his fancies.

He would pick up a thought here, an oddity there and run them all together. The finished necklace was like those chains of queerly sorted charms made by squaw women.

"Al," he turned to me with indolent deliberation, attempting to conceal the anxiety in his mind, "was he guilty?"

It was the thought tormenting me at that very moment. Neither of us had been thinking of another thing all evening.

"Colonel, the horror of this day has made an old man of me. Every hour I could feel that softy's freckled hand on my arm. I could see his gentle eyes smiling into mine. I believe him. I think he was innocent. Do you?

"You have seen many face death. A man might persist in a lie. But would a boy like that—a child keep at it so?"

"Nearly every man who has not pleaded guilty insists on his innocence to his last breath. I don't know about the Kid. He may have been speaking the truth. I felt that he was innocent."

"Good God, Al—What a frightful thing if they have murdered a boy and he was not guilty! The terrible insolence of men to convict on circumstantial evidence! Does it not prove the conceit of Thought?

"There can be no certainty to second-hand evidence —what right have we then to inflict an irrevocable penalty? The evidence may be disproved; the charges may be withdrawn, but the condemned may not be summoned back from the grave. It is monstrous. The arrogance of human beings must tempt the patience of God.

"I am right, colonel, for all your opposition, thought not poised with humility, is but a goad lashing man's conceit to madness or at the other extreme we have thought unblended with faith—then it is but a bludgeon striking man's yearnings down to despondency."

Abruptly he came over to me. He had picked up another bead for his fantastic chain.

"Was there ever a case in this pen when a man was electrocuted and it was afterward found that he was innocent?"

"Not in my time, Bill. But they tell of several. The old stir bugs could freeze the marrow in your bones with their tales."

"Some of them must be true. It is inconceivable that man's judgment should always be correct. The fact that one man has been cut off from life on evil evidence is sufficient indictment against the whole system of murder on circumstantial proof. How can men sit on a jury and take into their hands such wicked power?"

Several hours before the 9 o'clock gong had sounded there was a thick hush over the sleeping institution. Porter's whispering eloquence had lulled into quiet. Our uneasy pangs were well diluted in Tipo and into our harried minds there had drifted a half-dozing contentment. Suddenly a hoarse, rumbling growl that lifted into a piercing shriek came rasping out from the cell block.

Porter leaped to his feet.

"What was that? I was dreaming. It sounded like the crack of doom to me. This infernal place is haunted. I wonder if the Kid's spirit rests easily tonight? Colonel, do you believe in spirits, in an after life, in a God?"

"No, I don't—leastwise, I don't think I do."

"Well, I do in a way. I think there is some kind of an all-powerful spirit, but the God of humanity doesn't loiter in this pen. He doesn't seem to be a student of criminology.

"If I thought much about this affair of today I would lose all faith, all happiness. I would never be able to write a hopeful line."

It was well for Porter that his release was due in a short time. The world could not afford to miss the buoyancy of his faith.

He was not in the prison when the shocking truth came out. The Press Post carried the story, bringing out again all the facts in the case. Bob Whitney, the boy whose body was supposed to have been washed up from the Scioto, turned up in Portsmouth. He wrote to his parents. He knew nothing about the Kid's execution.

The State had made a little mistake. It had bumped off a boy of 17 for a murder that was never committed. It had thought the Kid was guilty.

CHAPTER XXV.

Last days of O. Henry in prison; intimate details; his going away outfit; goodbys; his departure.

The last leaf on the calendar was turned. Porter had but seven days more to serve. Even Billy grew quiet. When Porter came to the post-office, we would wait on him, yielding him the only comfortable chair, kicking a foot-stool under his feet. And once Billy grabbed up a pillow from his cot and stuffed it under Porter's head. Porter stretched his ample body and turned on Billy a cherubic smile.

"Gee, Bill, I ain't a gonna die, am I? Feel my pulse."

It was like that—funny—but under the burlesque was the disturbing sadness of farewell. We were full of idiotic consideration for Porter as people are when they feel that a friend is leaving them forever.

We were packing a suitcase of memories for him to carry along into the open world, hoping he might turn to it now and again with a thought for the two cons left in the prison post-office.

Goodbys are almost always one-sided, as though fate offered a toast—and the one who goes drinks off the wine and hands the glass with the dregs to the one who stays behind.

A twinge of regret Porter felt in the parting, perhaps, but it sent only a tremendous quiver through the buoyant swell of his joy in the thought of freedom. He was excited and full of a nervous gaiety. His whispering, hesitant voice took on a chirp and his serene face was jaunty with happiness.

"Colonel, I want you to do me a favor. I don't mind an obligation to you. I'll never pay it back and you won't hold it against me. You see, Al, I'm worried. I don't want to get arrested for running around unclad. And that's what might happen if you don't lend your valuable aid.

"It's this way. The stuff they make the going-away suits with goes away too quickly. It melts in the sun and if it should rain it dissolves. A man has no protection nohow.

"Now, when I came to this institution I brought a fine tweed suit with me. I'd like it back as a sort of dowry. Will you look it up for me, please? I do not admire prison gray. I'm afraid it is not a fashionable color this summer."

The large, humorous mouth—the one feature that was a bit weak—grinned. Porter buttoned his coat and surveyed himself sideways with the air of a dandy. A sheepish light stole into his eye.

"I feel like a bride getting a trousseau. I'm so particular about the sendoff this paternal roof is going to give me."

Porter's old suit had been given away to some other out-going convict.

"Use your influence, colonel, and get me a good-looking business suit. I'll leave it to your judgment, but pick me out a rich brown."

The superintendents of all the shops knew the secre-

tary of the steward's office. They were all fond of
the nimble-tongued, amiable dignity that was Bill
Porter's. Everyone wanted to make him a present as
he was leaving.

"Porter goin' on his honeymoon? Sure pick out
the best we've got. Harry Ogle was the outside super-
intendent of the State shop. He led me over to the
storeroom and pulled down bolt after bolt of fine
wool cloth.

The regulation convict suit was made of some cotton
mixture. The government paid the state $25 to clothe
its outgoing prisoners. The raiment was worth about
$4.50.

"Here's the finest piece of brown English worsted
in the State of Ohio." We decided on that and Porter
came over for a fitting. The men laughed as they
measured him.

"Want the seams runnin' crostwise just to be otherwise," they twitted. "If you had the pockets turned
upside down, they'd never git wise to where this handsome suit come from. And you ain't got nuthin' to
put in the pockets, anyways, and you'd be sure not to
come back as a sneak thief."

It would have hurt Porter's pride at another time,
but he was so concerned with the multitude of small
preparations he laughed and bandied back the crude
jests of the prison tailors. In return they fashioned
a suit that was without fault, even to Porter's
fastidious taste.

On the night of July 23—the next morning he was
to leave—Porter smuggled over his outfit.

"Gentlemen, whenever a great drama is to be

staged, it is customary to give a dress rehearsal. Let the curtain up."

Bill tried on the suit. He had a black Katy hat like the derby worn today and a pair of shoes made by a life termer. Prison shoes squeak. They can be heard a mile off. The cons used to say it was due on purpose to prevent a silent getaway. Porter's were no exception.

"I'll make quite a noise in the world, colonel. I'm bringing my own brass band along."

"You're bound to make a noise there, Bill."

"Here, try some of this hair tonic on them." Billy got down Porter's remedy. "It can take the kick out of anything."

Flippant, meaningless banter — we spent the precious hours flipping it back and forth. It was like the empty foam tossed from great waves against an impregnable rock. The waves themselves come with a mighty rush, but at the base of the crag they ebb as though their force were suddenly spent.

Thoughts and a hundred anxious questions were pushing upward in a surge of emotions, but at the tongue they failed and we dashed out this froth. We talked of everything but our thoughts.

Even the warden was nervous when Porter came into the office for his discharge.

"I worked them all night, colonel," Porter pointed to the shoes. "Their eloquence is irrepressible."

"If you looked any better, Bill, the ladies would kidnap you for a Beau Brummel."

"I shall not be taken into captivity again on any charge."

Porter's face was slightly lined. He looked older for his 39 months in prison, but even so, his was a head and a bearing to attract attention anywhere. There was about him now an attitude of confidence, or self-sufficiency, of dignity. He looked more like a well-educated, cultured business man than like an ex-convict.

There were visitors in the outer office. The warden stepped outside, telling me to give Bill his discharge papers. As soon as we were alone the intense strain became unbearable. I wanted to cram everything into those last moments. I wanted to say: "Good luck—God bless you—Go to hell."

But neither of us spoke. Bill went over to the window and I sat down to the desk. For 10 minutes he stood there. Suddenly it occurred to me that he was taking this parting in a very indifferent manner.

"Bill," my voice was husky with resentment and he turned quickly; "won't you be outside soon enough? Can't you look this way for the last few minutes we've got?"

The coaxing smile on his lips, he put out his strong, short hand to me. "Al, here's a book, I sent to town for it for you." It was a copy of "Omar Khayyam." I handed him the discharge and his $5. Porter had at least $60 or $70—the proceeds from his last story. He took the $5.

"Here, colonel, give this to Billy—he can buy alcohol for his locomotor ataxia."

That was all. He went toward the door and then he came back the old drollery in his eye.

"I'll meet you in New York, colonel. You might

beat the brakes there before me. I'll be on the watch. Goodby, Al."

Porter's voice lapsed into a low whisper at the end. He went to the door, and, without looking back, went out. I felt as though something young and bonny— something lovable and magnetic—was gone forever.

"No leaves on the calendar, Al!" Billy Raidler scratched off the last number, shook his head and tore off the page. He looked over at me through a gloom of silence.

"Another day gone into night."

CHAPTER XXVI.

O. Henry's silence; a letter at last; the proposed story; Mark Hanna visits the prison; pardon; double-crossed; freedom.

Egotism is the bridge whereon men have crawled upward from the jungle. There is no limit to its reaches. It spans even the heavens, paving the way to gods and angels, whose sole delight is to minister to men. It is not stopped even at the grave, but flings a tight rope beyond, and on this hair line Man marches to Immortality. Without Egotism, the human animal never would have developed.

Across one chasm it does not stretch—the chasm between the World and Prison. And in this exile the convict becomes spiritless and hopeless. He expects nothing, for he has lost the self-esteem that buoys trust.

When Bill Porter went down the walk to the Open Road in his squeaky shoes and the arrogant yellow gloves Steve Bussel had given him, neither Billy Raidler nor I ever expected to catch again an echo from those familiar footsteps. He had sauntered out of our lives. We were glad for the sunny companionship he had given us when he was one with ourselves.

We talked about him now and then, Billy always brought up the conversation.

"I need some tobacco—a special brand—think I'll drop a line to Bill Porter and ask him to send it on." Or again, it was his hair that worried him. "Fool that I was—I forgot to get that remedy from Bill. I'm like to be bald before he sends his address. Say, Al, didn't he promise to give you a lift on the story—what about it?"

But the weeks went by and no word came. A month and a half to the day Billy sent a runner to the warden's office with a letter postmarked "Pittsburgh." The runner brought a note from Raidler: "Al, send me back that letter. My locomotor ataxia is itchin' to see what Bill's got to say. Yours in great peril, Billy."

Here is the first letter Bill Porter—he had already taken the name of O. Henry—had sent to me at the Ohio penitentiary. He had not forgotten us and he had already made good:

"Dear Jennings: I have intended to write to you and Billy every week since I left, but kept postponing it because I expected to move on to Washington (sounds like Stonewall Jackson talk, doesn't it?) almost any time. I am very comfortably situated here, but expect to leave in a couple of weeks, anyhow.

"I have been doing quite a deal of business with the editors since I got down to work and have made more than I could at any other business. I want to say that Pittsburgh is the 'low-downedest' hole on the surface of the earth. The people here are the most ignorant, ill-bred, contemptible, boorish, degraded, insulting, sordid, vile, foul-mouthed, indecent, profane, drunken, dirty, mean, depraved curs that I ever imagined could exist. Columbus people are models of chivalry compared with them. I shall linger here no longer than necessary.

"Besides, on general principles, I have a special object in writing to you just now. I have struck up quite a correspondence with the editor of Everybody's Magazine. I have sold him two articles in August and have orders for others. In writing to him some time ago I suggested an article with a title something like 'The Art and Humor of Holding Up a Train,' telling him that I thought I could get it written by an expert in the business.

"Of course, I mentioned no names or localities. He seemed very much struck with the idea and has written twice asking about it. The only fear he had, he said, was that the expert would not put it in a shape suitable for publication in Everybody's as John Wanamaker was very observant of the proprieties.

"Now, if you would care to turn yourself loose on the subject there may be something in it and a start on future work besides. Of course, you needn't disclose your identity in the slightest degree. What he wants (as I thought he would) is a view of the subject from the operator's standpoint.

"My idea would be a chatty sort of article—just about the way you usually talk, treating it descriptively and trying out the little points and details, just as a man would talk of his chicken farm or his hog ranch.

"If you want to tackle it, let me know and I'll send you my idea of the article, with all the points that should be touched upon. I will either go over it and arrange it according to my conception of the magazine requirements, or will forward your original MS., whichever you prefer. Let me know soon, as I want to answer his letter.

"Well how is the P. O. and vice versa? It's an awful job for me to write a letter. I believe my pencil handwriting is nearly as bad as yours.

"One letter to Harris is the best I've accomplished in the way of correspondence since I left. I haven't written to Louisa in two months. I hope she don't feel grieved. I am going to write her pretty soon.

"If I could get 30 days in the O. P. I believe I'd crack one of the statues that much to get a change of society from the hounds here. I'd rather sit in the dumphouse there and listen to the bucket lids rattle than to hear these varmints talk, as far as entertainment is concerned.

"Pard, they don't get no lowdowneder than the air here. If I could just have that black coon that comes in the P. O. every night with a tin bucket to run with here instead of Pittsburglars, I'd be much better satisfied.

"Give Billy R. my profoundest respects. Tell him he's more pumpkins than the whole population of Pennsylvania rolled into one man, not excluding John Wanamaker's Sunday school class. May the smoke of his cigarettes ascend forever.

"Write me as soon as you feel like it and I assure you I will be glad to hear from you. I am surrounded by wolves and fried onions, and a word from one of the salt of the earth will come like a clap of manna

from a clear roof garden. Remember me to Messrs.
Ira Maralatt and Star (D. J.).

"Sincerely yours,   W. S. P."

In less than two months the road from prison forked
into the road to fame for Bill Porter. The plans he
had made matured. He set resolutely to his work.
"Behold me, the lazy man Louisa used to guy,"
he said in a second letter, "averaging $150 a month.
I always knew they didn't know laziness from dignified
repose."

That letter from Porter did more than restore trust
in a friend. It gave me a foothold on the great bridge.
Self-confidence and hope leaped into quivering
vitality. Bill Porter believed I could make good. He
was holding out a hand to me.

I set to work that night. Billy held the pens. We
were the kind who "dash off stories" that editors dash
back. It was nearly morning when the first draft of
the "holdup" was ready for mail.

Our Fate drives onward like a snowball—gathering
momentum with every act. Some deed that is but a
flake drops across the current of our lives and before
we are aware of it the flake has doubled, tripled its
size. A thousand kindred flakes flutter down to meet
it until the tremendous force gathers itself together
and rushes us to our Destiny.

It seemed to be this way with me, Porter's letter
was the first incident—another and another came pre-
cipitately. A new outlook was before me.

We sent the outline of the story to Porter. In two
days we had an answer.

"Dear Pard—Your prompt reply was received this morning and read with pleasure. I assure you it is always a joyful thing for a man in Pittsburgh to be reminded of the O. P. It is like Lazarus in H—— looking up and seeing the rich men order a schooner.

"Am I then so much in love with the O. P.? No, my son, I am speaking comparatively. I am only trying to put the royal skibunk onto Pittsburgh. The only difference between P. and O. P. is that they are allowed to talk at dinner here. . . ."

With the most illuminating detail, Porter went on to give me the directions for writing the story. I used my first experience in train-robbery—the stickup of the M. K. T. That letter was a lesson in short-story writing. It showed the unlimited pains O. Henry took to make his work the living reality it is.

He neglected nothing—character, setting, atmosphere, traits, slang—all were considered; all must be in harmony with the theme. I spoke of this letter in connection with the chapter on my first expedition with the outlaws. It served as a model outline for me in my future attempts.

When the story was finished Billy and I went over it. Billy demanded that real blood be shed just to give it color, but I stuck to the facts. The genuine outlaw kills only when his own life is at stake.

"It's a wonder, anyway, Al—gee whiz—you and Bill will be no end famous."

Porter revised the narrative, slashed it, added to it, put the kick in it—made it a story. We waited a month for an answer. And in the mean time, Fate was busy.

For three years my father and my brother John had worked persistently for the commutation of my sentence. They had many influential friends. Frank was still in Leavenworth. His term was but five years. I had worked up a following with the wealthy contractors. Some of them took a liking to me. They promised to pull the wires to win my release. All at once, our combined efforts seemed to have produced a result.

I was filling out requisitions in the warden's office. A big, corpulent man, bluff, hardy, but likable, walked into the room. He seemed to fill up the entire space. I don't believe the Lord Himself would have given out such an all-pervading impression. The man was Mark Hanna.

"Where is the warden?" he asked. "Out," I answered.

"I'm looking for a man by the name of Jennings."

"I presume I'm the man," I answered with great dignity. "That's my name."

Hanna sent an appraising glance from the top of my fiery head to my well-shined boots. He brushed out his hand as though flecking me out of his mind as a man might a fly from his wrist.

"Well, you're not the Jennings I'm looking for. This fellow was a train-robbing s———— in the Indian Territory."

"I'm all of that except the s————."

The heavy fellow laughed until his jowls shook.

"Why, you're no bigger than a shrimp and just about that red."

Even from a Senator this raillery was a bit insolent.

I didn't exactly like it. "Senator, a Colt's forty-five makes all men equal." Hanna seemed greatly amused. The warden came in.

"Who is this atom?" he asked. Darby entered at once into Hanna's merriment.

"The gentleman was a train-robber by profession. His name is Jennings. His career met with a sad interruption and now he is detained here by the government for life."

Hanna evidently had the school boy's idea of the bandit. He was prepared to see a six-footer with a tough mug where a human face should be and the mark of all damnation in his mouth and eye. He couldn't reconcile my five-foot four with the picture. But he sat down and we began to talk. I became voluble. I told him a hundred odd escapades of the outlaw days. It seemed to entertain him.

"You're a likable microbe. I've heard of you from very reliable sources. I believe you are straight, I'll speak to Mr. McKinley about you. He is the kindest man in the world. We'll get you out."

The promise raised me to almost hysterical hilarity. I could think of nothing but freedom. I imagined I would be turned loose perhaps the next day—surely within a week. I wrote to Porter telling him I would see him within the fortnight. We could collaborate on another story. (For Porter had been generous enough to call me a collaborator for the "dope" on the holdup.) He wrote back.

"Great news," he said. "Hanna can do it. He made the President and he has a chattel mortgage on the United States."

The fortnight came. Porter sent an urgent query. "Why didn't you show up, colonel? I had the schooners chartered." In the same letter he told me that the story as he had revised it had been accepted by *Everybody's*. The check would be sent on publication.

"As soon as the check comes, I'll send you your 'sheer of the boodle.' By the way, please keep my nom de plume strictly to yourself. I don't want anyone to know just yet.

"P. S.—Did you get a little book on short story writing? The reason I ask, I had a store order it and they were to send it direct to you. You have to watch these damn hellions here or they'll do you for 5 cents."

The story-writing kept my mind occupied in the months of waiting for the promised commutation. At last a telegram came! I would be free.

They were anxious, straining days—in that week before my discharge. Hopes, ambitions, old ideals—they went like tireless phantoms before my eyes. Waking or sleeping, I had but one thought—"I must make good—I've got to get back—I'll show them all."

It was the morning of my release. Warden Darby met me in the corridor.

"Walk over to the hospital with me, Al." Darby's face was mottled grey—it got that way whenever he was laboring under excitement or anger.

"By God, Al, I hate to tell you!"

I stood still—the hot blood pounding into my throat, my ears. I felt as though the flesh were drop-

ping from my bones in a kind of throbbing terror.
Was my father dead? Was John dead?

"They've done you a damn' scurvy trick, Al. The
United States marshal is waiting for you. They're
going to take you to Leavenworth for five years
more."

Five years more in prison! It might as well have
been fifty. A blighting tornado of rage overswept
me, whipping out every new hope, every honest
thought. I felt lashed and tormented as though the
blood in my veins were suddenly turned into a million
scorpions, stinging me to a hot fury of blinding madness.

I rushed into the post-office, dashed the neat bundle
of treasures I had gathered to the ground. Photo-
graphs of some of the "cons"—a steel watch fob a
"lifer" in the contract shop made for me, an old
wooden box fashioned by a "stir-bug" in the lumber
mills—these and a few other things I had wrapped
together. I wanted these mementoes. Billy looked
at me and the trinkets strewn to the floor.

"Don't seem to be too chipper, Al. Ain't sorry to
kick the dust of the O. P. off your boots, be ye?"

I was kneeling on the floor, dumping the treasure
into a big handkerchief and dumping them out again,
scarcely conscious of the repetition. I was afraid to
talk, afraid even to look at Billy. A murderous hatred
was rearing like an angry snake in my mind.

Before I was aware of it Billy had shuffled over to
me, helping himself along with the chair. He sat
down, grabbed the bundle out of my hands and tied
it up.

"What hit you, Al?"

"Double-crossed. 'Tain't New York, 'tain't Oklahoma, it's Leavenworth for me—five years."

I spat the words out in a vicious gust. Billy dropped the bundle, his mouth sagged open. Amazed and unbelieving, he stared at me.

"Can't be true, Al. They're kiddin' you."

I took the bundle from him. "The marshal is waiting for me!" I started running from the room.

"Al, you ain't going without sayin' goodby?" Billy's crippled spine kept him from reaching me. I turned back. He stretched out his slender hand. He was crying. "It's a damn' shame, Al."

I went outside into a warm flood of sunshine. There was a zip and a dash in the air and the flowers seemed to flaunt their jaunty spring colors. If I had been free I would have gulped in that buoyant gladness in the air.

I was doomed, and the slap in the soft breezes put only an added tang to the bitterness in my heart. The marshal's long, black figure leaned against a stone column just outside the gates. He was twirling something that glittered in his hands.

As I came near him he took a step toward me, dangling the handcuffs. Something insane, unreasoning as a tiger, possessed me. I made a leap. The marshal drew back. We faced each other, both ready to spring. And then Darby, breathless and flurried, was between us.

"Don't handcuff him! He's straight as a die." The marshal, already weak with fear, dropped the steel rings into his pocket. "He won't try to escape."

For the entire trip he made no attempt to guard me. I made no effort to escape. At Leavenworth he turned me over to the warden. The shame and the ignominy of going again through the measurements, the mugging, the head-shaving, of standing again in the fourth-grade criminal class, humiliated me with a mean, paltry, slap-in-the-face kind of feeling.

I had no interest left in life. Not even the thought of seeing Frank buoyed me.

I felt too degraded to wish for the meeting. It was a silent, mournful reunion two pals had. Frank looked at me and I at him, and we didn't say a word until the guard beckoned for me to leave.

Something had died in me. After that I saw very little of my brother. I didn't even try to see him. Six months of weary, sordid stagnation wheeled along.

And then one morning, with but a breath of warning, the light broke for me. I walked out of the pen.

John and my father had pressed my case. The United Circuit Court of Appeals released me on a writ of habeas corpus. The court ruled that my imprisonment in Leavenworth was illegal and that the verdict which sentenced me to five years was worthless, as I had received this term on top of a sentence to life.

I had been convicted in one county and given life for the Rock Island train-robbery. I had been immediately whisked to another district and given five years for assault on Marshal Bud Ledbetter. The court ruled that this district had no jurisdiction over me at the time the sentence was imposed.

When they told me I was free it was as immaterial

to me as though they had ordered me to carry a message from one cell block to another.

Six months before Billy Raidler and I had sat far into the night discussing my future. Should I go to New York and try to write, make a fortune and return to the home folks?

Should I dash back to them dead broke and trust to luck for success?

These problems did not exist for me now. I had fallen into a kind of lethargy. I had written to no one. I had put far away every ambition and plan for the "come back." I was a sort of animated corpse.

Not until I stood at the door of Frank's cell and he put out his hand and looked down at me did a tremor of emotion seize me. My brother started to speak. His words were muffled and indistinct. He held my hand.

"For God's sake, Al, let her be on the square from now on!" It came out blurting, anxious, pleading. An overpowering tide of remorse swept over me. I'd have given the soul out of my body to have changed places with him.

CHAPTER XXVII.

Practice of law; invitation from O. Henry; visit to Roosevelt; citizenship rights restored; with O. Henry in New York; the writer as guide.

It was on the square with me. I went back to Oklahoma and took up the practice of law. After a year of temptation, hardship and starving in a land of plenty I began to make good. One case followed another. I had a few big successes.

Several years passed. I had all but forgotten Bill Porter. One morning a big, square envelope came through the mails. The moment I glanced at that clear, fine handwriting something seemed to reach into me and grab me by the heart.

I felt a bubbling happiness singing as it had not in years. I could hear the whispering music of Bill Porter's voice lisping across the continent.

That letter came early in 1905. Porter urged me to write. The old ambition flared up. I started again on the "Night Riders." It was the beginning of a long correspondence. And then came a letter:

"Algie Jennings, The West, Dear Al: Got your message all right. Hope you'll follow it soon. Well, as I had nothing to do, I thought I would write you a letter and as I have nothing to say I will now close (joke)."

The letter rambled through four delicious pages of

whimsicality, each urging me in a different vein to visit New York. When I finished it I started to pack my trunk.

Bill Porter was already a celebrity in New York. He was O. Henry, the man endeared to a million hearts for his stories in "The Four Million," "The Voice of the City," and four other equally famous collections. The thought of visiting this glorified Bill thrilled me.

But I had another motive in making the trip. I was going to make a stop-over in Washington. I decided to call on Theodore Roosevelt at the White House. I wanted a full and free pardon. I wanted to be restored to citizenship.

No triumph in the courtroom had ever dulled my pride on this score. Every time I passed an election booth and saw other men casting their ballots I was stung with humiliation.

Since my release from Leavenworth I had worked incessantly toward regaining my rights. The biggest Republican in Oklahoma had spoken for me. I decided to make my plea personally to the greatest of them all. Sheer gall won me that audience—unbiased fairness on the part of the President made the mission a success.

John Abernathy was United States marshal in Oklahoma. He was a hunter. When Roosevelt had come to the State Abernathy was his wolf-catcher. Between the two men there was a deep, sincere affection. Abernathy was a friend of mine. He agreed to make the trip and present my case to President Roosevelt.

We had managed to get ourselves into the Cabinet
room. Five or six men were standing around filling
up the moments of waiting with lusty chatter. Only
one of them I recognized—Joe Cannon. Abernathy
and I stood in one corner, as futile and helpless as
two little buttermilk calves trying to find shelter from
the rain.

I kept my glance fastened on a door. "He'll come
through that one," I thought. But when the door shot
open with a vigorous push and the Great Man came
swinging in, the shock of excited emotion bewildered
me.

Roosevelt's presence seemed to tingle through the
room as though a vivid current of electricity were
suddenly conducted from one to another. It was the
first time I had ever seen him. He looked as though
he had come up from a stimulating swim, as though
every drop of blood throbbed with eager health.

The quivering exuberance of youth met the rugged
strength of maturity in the abounding personality
standing in the middle of the Cabinet room. He saw
every man at a glance. He ignored practically all but
Abernathy.

"Hello, John!" The tense hand reached out. "How
are the wolves down in Oklahoma?" He swept
around. Roosevelt didn't walk or step; there was too
much spontaneity, too much vitality in every gesture
for such prosy motions. "This, gentlemen, is my
United States marshal, John Abernathy of Oklahoma."

"Mr. President, this is my friend, Al Jennings,"
the wolf-catcher replied.

Roosevelt's quick, boring eyes turned on me. "I'm glad to see you sir. I know what you want. I'm a very busy man. I'll have to see you later."

"Mr. President," the words catapulted out of my mouth, "I'll never get in here again. My business is more important to me than your Cabinet meeting. I want to be a citizen of the United States again."

The snapping light of humor came into the eyes, and at once Roosevelt seemed to me to have the shrewdest, kindest, most tolerant expression I had ever seen. He seemed to be taking a whimsically measured appraisement of me.

"I think you're right, sir. Citizenship is greater in this country of ours than a Cabinet meeting." He turned to the men. "Gentlemen, excuse me a moment. You'll have to wait."

In the private room near where the Cabinet met Roosevelt sat on the edge of a desk. "I want to know," he shot out abruptly, "if you were guilty of the crime you went to prison for."

"No, sir."

"You were not there then?"

"I was there, I held up the train and robbed the passengers." The relentlessly honest eyes never took their glance from mine. "But I did not rob the United States mail, and that's what I was convicted for."

"That's a distinction without a difference." The words were snapped out with incisive clearness.

"It's the truth, however, I'll tell you nothing, Mr. President, but the truth."

"Abernathy and Frank Frans have assured me you

would tell only the truth. I have studied your case.
I am going to give you a full and free pardon. I
want you to be worthy of it."

It would have been ended then. But the devil of
perversity that had so often loosened my tongue
whisked me to the absurd folly of replying. I had
no sense of the proprieties.

"Mr. President, the court that sentenced me was
more guilty of violating the law than I was. Judge
Hosea Townsend won the verdict from the jury by
trickery."

If I had suddenly gone up and slapped his face,
Roosevelt would not have sprung down with more
flashing indignation. A red flurry of anger scooted
across his face. He scowled down at me, the even
teeth showing. I thought he was going to strike me.
I had said too much. I'd have given an eye to own
the words again.

"You have brought charges against one of my
appointees." His voice was even and quiet. "You
will have to substantiate this."

I thought the pardon was lost. I told him the facts.

Ten jurors had testified under oath that Marshal
Hammer of the Southern District of Indian Territory
had come into the jury room when they were de-
liberating the evidence in my case and he had told
them Judge Townsend would give me the lightest
sentence under the law if they would return a verdict
of guilty. Under the impression that I would be
given a year, they voted me guilty. The next morning
Townsend sentenced me for life to the Ohio penitentiary.

My brother John had secured these affidavits. They were on file in the attorney general's office. I told the President this.

He never said a word, but went to the door and gave some hasty order. Then he came back, walking furiously up and down the room, holding himself stiff and clenched.

It seemed to me that I could feel the vibrating anger in his mind. Some word came back from the outer room.

"You are a truth-teller," Roosevelt turned to me. "The pardon is yours. Be worthy of it. I wish you good luck."

He seemed borne down by suppressed emotion. He offered me his hand. I was so touched I could scarcely mumble my thanks. A free man and a citizen, I landed in New York to meet Bill Porter.

I had counted too much on Bill Porter's fame. I knew that New York was a big place, but I had an idea that Porter would tower above the crowd like a blond Hercules in a city of dwarfs.

Abernathy and I had rollicked along from Washington to New York. When the boat swung down the Hudson we didn't know whether we were en route to Liverpool or Angel Island. But we did know that we were looking for one Bill Porter. I had lost the letter giving me his address.

We wandered up one street and down another, a queer-looking pair with our wide fedora hats. Every now and then I made bold and plucked the sleeve of some man, woman or child. "Hey, pard, can you tell me where Bill Porter lives?" They stared coldly and passed on. I heard one young fellow titter, "The poor babes from the woods."

We couldn't find Bill.

But we were in an irrepressibly happy mood. With not the slightest idea how we got there we landed at the Breslin Hotel. We began to treat everybody at the bar.

The whole crowd knew the Outlaw and the Wolf-Catcher were in town.

"By golly, we haven't found Bill." Abernathy smashed his glass down on the counter.

"Bill who?" the bartender asked.

"Bill Porter. Know him, greatest man in New York?"

"Sure, know them all."

"Let's telephone to the President and ask him where this fellow lives. He's a good sport; he'll send us a pilot." Abernathy's "hunch" gave me a better one. Dr. Alex Lambert, physician to Roosevelt, had shown us many courtesies. He lived in New York. We decided to use him as our guide if we could find him.

I remembered that Porter lived near Gramercy Park. I phoned to the doctor and with the utmost formality asked directions to this district. The absurdity of the question didn't seem to amaze him. He went into elaborate details.

Arm in arm, Abernathy and I sauntered to the park and with the most painful dignity went up the steps of every house and rang the bell, inquiring for Bill Porter. Not a soul had ever heard of him. Somehow or other we strayed into the Players' Club. The

flunkies didn't like the cut of our clothes. We had to
bribe them before they would admit us.

"Where is Mr. William Sydney Porter, the
writer?" I asked one of them.

"Didn't know; never heard of him. Ask him over
there. He knows even the small fry. He's Bob
Davis."

The chunky little fellow with his ample, humorous
face and his keen gray eyes, was standing at the door
of a big meeting room. I went up to him.

"Are you acquainted with Bill Porter?"

"Never heard of the gentleman." He didn't even
shift his glance toward me. "My circle embraces only
writers, waiters and policemen."

And then I remembered who it was I was looking
for.

"Oh, thank you." I tried to make my voice very
casual. "Do you happen to know a man by the name
of O. Henry?" The little fellow's face lit up like an
arc lamp. His hand swooped down on mine. "Do I?
I should say so. Do you?"

"Me!" I fairly screamed at him. "Hell, yes, he's
an old pal of mine."

"So? What part of the West does he come from?"
The editor's scrutiny took in even the freckles on my
hand. Porter had them guessing already. They would
not learn his secret from me. For a moment I did
not answer.

"He's from the South," I said finally. "Do you
know where I can find him?"

"Ring up the Caledonia Hotel, 28 West Twenty-
sixth Street."

Porter was found at last.

"Is that you, colonel?" The same old rich, suspenseful flavor in the whispering voice. "I'll be with you anon. God bless you."

In a very short "anon" in came the immaculate, flawless Bill as though something adventurous and exciting had just happened to him or were just about to happen. He wore a handsome gray suit, with a rich blue tie, the everlasting glove and cane in his right hand.

"Hey, Bill, why don't you carry a forty-five instead of that trinket?"

"Colonel, the forty-five is not fashionable just now. And there are folks in Manhattan who object to the custom, notably the Legislature."

Just as though it had been five minutes since I had spoken to him instead of five years! With all his warm, fine-tempered affection, he stood silent and searched my face.

"It's you, colonel. Ain't spoiled, are you?"

We sat down to a table, ordered a drink, forgot to drink it and sat there shaking each other's hand and nodding to each other like a pair of mutes.

"How are Hans and Fritz?" Porter's voice was charged with feeling. Yet the twins were but a pair of prison kittens born and raised in the post-office.

Like a pair of farmer boys who had grown up together, ducked in the same creek and gone to the little school on Ball Knob, we sat back swapping reminiscences of the hated, horror-haunted O. P.

"It's good you've been there', colonel. It's the proper vestibule to this City of Damned Souls. The

crooks there are straight compared to the business
thieves here. If you've got $2 on you, invest it now
or they'll take it away from you before morning."

It was midnight when we started down to the old
Hoffman House for a farewell toast. We were to
meet early next morning for our first survey of the
little village. Abernathy and I were up at six. Porter
came over at eleven. The first feature on his entertainment program was a joyride on a "rubberneck
wagon."

"You'll get a swift, fleeting glimpse of this Bagdad
and its million mysteries. You'll see the princess in
disguise glide past the street corners evading evil
genii; meeting with grand viziers. Keep your eyes
open."

Abernathy, Porter and I were the only passengers.
In a raucous sing-song the guide shouted. "To your
right, gentlemen, is the home of Sheridan Land," or
some such cognomen. "And further down to your
left is the tomb of Grant."

Porter fidgeted. He got up and handed the cicerone
a $2 bill. "Keep your tongue in your cheek," he said
impressively. "We are neither entomologists interested in gold bugs nor antiquarians hob-nobbing with
the dead. We are children of Bacchus. Lead us to
the curb."

It was a cold, raw day. Cicerone, wolf-catcher, outlaw, genius, we took many side trips to the haunts of
our father. The driver became reckless and jammed
into a street car. For a moment it looked as if we
would all be "pinched." Abernathy and I wanted to
"mix it with the cop."

"Restrain yourselves, gentlemen. I will straighten the legal tangle." With commanding elegance, Porter stepped down, threw open his coat and showed some sort of star. The policeman apologized. It seemed a miracle to us.

"He is the magician of Bagdad," I whispered to Abernathy. In the next three weeks he proved it. Bill Porter waved his hand and his "Bagdad on the Subway" yielded its million mysteries to the touch.

CHAPTER XXVIII

Episodes of city nights; feeding the hungry; Mame and Sue; suicide of Sadie.

Night was the revealing hour for the magician of Bagdad. When the million lights flashed and throngs of men and women crowded the thoroughfares in long, undulating lines like moving, black snakes, Bill Porter came into his own.

He owned the city, its people were his subjects. He went into their midst, turning upon them the shrewd microscope of his gleaming understanding. Sham, paltry deceit, flimsy pose, were blown away as veils before a determined wind. The souls stood forth, naked and pathetic. The wizard had his way.

At every corner, adventure waited on his coming. A young girl would skim stealthily around the corner, or an old "win" would crouch in a doorway. Here were mysteries for Porter to solve. He did not stand afar and speculate. He always made friends with his subjects.

He learned their secrets, their hopes, their disappointments. He clasped the hand of Soapy, the bum, and Dulcie herself told him why she went totally bankrupt on six dollars a week. New York was an enchanted labyrinth, yielding at every twist the thrill of the unexpected—the wonderful.

Into this kingdom of his, Bill Porter introduced me.

Jaunty, whimsical, light-hearted, he came for me one of the first nights of my visit. He wore a little Cecil Brunner rose in his buttonhole. With a sheepish wink, he pulled another from his pocket.

"Colonel, I have bought you a disguise. Wear this and they will not know you are from the West."

"Damn it, I don't want the garnishings." But when Bill had a notion he carried it out. The pink bud was fastened to my coat. "I've noticed that the bulls look at you with a too favorable eye. This token will divert suspicion from us."

"Where are we going?"

"Everywhere and nowhere. We may find ourselves in Hell's Kitchen or we may land in Heaven's Vestibule. Prepare yourself for thrills and perils. We go where the magnet draweth."

It was nearing midnight. We started down Fifth Avenue and were sauntering along somewhere between Twenty-fifth and Twenty-sixth. Dozens of women with white, garish faces had flitted by.

"Ships that pass in the night," Porter whispered. "There are but two rocks in their courses—the cops and their landladies. Battered and storm-tossed, aren't they? They haunt me."

Out from the shadow came a ragged wisp of a girl. She looked about 17.

"She's been skimming the tranquil bogs of country life."

"Aw, shucks, she's an old timer."

"First trip," Porter nudged me. She hasn't learned how to steer her bark in the deeps of city life yet."

"That's her game. She's just flying that sail for effect."

"No, you're mistaken. You investigate and we'll see who's correct. I'll stand here and hold the horses." Porter had a way of pulling things out of the past and snapping them at me.

As we came up, the girl dodged into a doorway, making a pretense of tying her shoe. She looked up at me, fright darting in her wide, young eyes. "You're a plainclothes man?" Her voice was low but it shrilled in her fear.

"Please don't take me in. I never did this before."

"I'm not a policeman, but I'd like to introduce you to a friend of mine."

Bill came over. "You've frightened the lady. Ask her if she would like to dine with us."

More frightened than before, the girl drew back. "I dare not go with you!"

"You dare go anywhere with us." Porter addressed her as though she were truly the princess and he the Knight Errant.

There was nothing personal in his interest. He had one indomitable passion—he wished to discover the secret and hidden things in the characters of the men and women about him. He wanted no second-hand or expurgated versions. He was a scientist and the quivering heart of humanity was the one absorbing subject under his scrutiny.

We went to Mouquin's. The little, thin, white creature had never been there before. Her eyes were luminous with excitement. Porter made her feel so much at ease, it disconcerted me a trifle. I wanted the girl to know that she was in the presence of greatness.

"He's a great writer," I whispered to her. Porter turned a withering sneer at me. "I'm nothing of the sort," he contradicted. "Oh, but I believe it," she said. "I'd like to see what you write. Is it about wonderful people and money and everything grand?"

"Yes," Porter answered. "It's about girls like you and all the strange things that happen to you."

"But my life isn't fine. It's just mean and scraping and hungry, and fine things never happened to me until tonight. Ever since I can remember it's been the same."

Porter had started her on the revelation. He was correct. She was but a little country girl. She had tired of the monotony and came to life.

There was nothing remarkable about her. I couldn't see a story there. The only spark she showed was when the dinner came and then a look of inspired joyousness lighted her face. It seemed to me that Porter must surely be disappointed.

"When I see a shipwreck, I like to know what caused the disaster," he said.

"Well, what did you make of that investigation?"

"Nothing but the glow that wrapped her face when the soup came! That's the story."

"What's behind that look of rapture? Why should any girl's face glow at the prospect of a plate of soup in this city, where enough food to feed a dozen armies is wasted every night? Yes, it's more of a story than will ever be written!"

Each one that he met yielded a treasure to him. Into the honkatonks, the dance halls, the basement cafés he took me. The same indomitable purposes guided him. No wonder that New York threw off its disguise before the Peerless Midnight Investigator.

"I scent an idea tonight, colonel. Let us go forth and track it down." It was another evening and I had dined with him at the Caledonia Hotel.

We started down Sixth Avenue. The rain splashed sideways and downways. Puny lights flickered up from basement doors. The mingled odor of stale beer, cabbage and beans simmered up. We went down into many of these paltry halls, with the sawdust on the floor and the chipped salt cellars and the scratched up, bare tables.

"It's not here. Let us go to O'Reilly's. I don't like the fragrance of these dago joints." At Twenty-second street Porter pulled down his umbrella. "We'll find it in here."

At the bar were a score of men. The tables here and there were but shelves for the elbows of gaudily dressed, cheaply jeweled women.

We took a vacant table. As Porter sat down every woman in the room sent an admiring glance at him.

"For God's sake, Bill, you won't eat in this stench, will you?"

"Just beer and a sandwich. Look over there, colonel. I see my idea."

In one corner sat two girls, pretty, shabby, genteel, the stark, piercing glare of hunger in their eyes. Porter beckoned to them.

The girls came over and sat at our table. It was the cheapest kind of a dance hall in this basement under the saloon. A fellow with an accordion was pounding a tune with an old rattle-bang piano; a few tawdry-looking couples moved with grotesque rhythm in the middle of the floor. At the tables about a score of men sat erect and stupid—some of them half drunk; others bawling out harsh snatches of songs. The noisy guffaw of the place was more disturbing than the reeking exhalation of its breath.

Porter handed the dirty scrap of paper that passed as a ménu to the girls. Their eyes seemed to pounce on it. One of them was rather gracefully built, but so thin I had the odd feeling that she might break at any moment like an egg shell. She tried to scan the card indifferently, but her cavernous eyes, their black accentuated by the daubs of rouge on the transparent cheeks, were burning with eagerness. She caught me looking at her and turned to the rather short, fair-haired girl at her side.

"Suppose you order, Mame." There was no pretense to Mame. She was hungry and she spotted a chance to eat. "Say, Mister," she leaned toward Porter, "can I order what I want?"

"I don't think you better. You see, ladies, I haven't the price." He ordered four beers.

I couldn't follow the drift of this experiment. Porter had picked out these two from the dozens of tell-tale painted faces. He knew his magic circle. But I didn't like the bore of hungry eyes. Mame was absorbed in watching a blowsy, puffy-cheeked woman amiably gathering in drippy spoonfuls of cabbage. It bothered me. I slipped my purse to Porter.

"My God, Bill, buy them a feed." He sneaked it back to me.

"Wait.   There's a story here."   He paid the bill. It was about 20 cents.   He spoke a moment to the manager.   Whatever he wanted, the manager was ready to give.

"Would you ladies like to come out and get a square meal?" Mame looked nervously about the room. Sue stood up. "Thank you," she said. "It would be quite agreeable."

We started toward the Caledonia Hotel, where Porter had his study. "We're making a mistake, Sue. We'll all get pinched. The instant we step into a hash house with these gents, the bulls'll nab us. We better beat it. We're makin' an awful mistake."

"We're nuthin' but mistakes anyhow. If there's a chance to eat I'm gonna take it." Sue's talk was a curious blend of dignity, bitterness and slang.

"You're making no mistake."

Porter led the way at a quick pace. "Where we are going the foot of a bull has never thumped."

It was after one o'clock when we reached the hotel. Porter ordered a beefsteak, potatoes, coffee, and a crab salad. He served it on the table where so many of his masterpieces were written. In that outlandish situation, with Mame sitting on a box, Sue in an easy chair, and Porter with a towel over his arm like a waiter serving us, one of those stories came into being that morning.

"Do you make much coin?" When he talked to them he was one of them. He adopted their language and their thought.

"Ain't nuthin' to be made."

Mame was stowing in the beefsteak and swallowing

it with scarcely a pause. "All we can git is enough to pay two dollars a week for a room. An' if we're lucky we eat and if we ain't we starve, 'cept we meet sporty gents like yerselves."

"You don't know what it is to be hungry," Sue added quietly. She was ravenously hungry, and it was with an obvious jerk of her will that she kept herself from the greedy quickness of Mame. "You ain't suffered as we have."

"I guess we ain't." Bill winked at me. "It's kind o' hard to get a footing here, I suppose."

"Well, you guessed it that time. Sure is. If you come through with yer skin, you're lucky. And if you're soft, you die." Sue sat back and looked at her long white hands.

"That's what Sadie done. Her and me come from Vermont together. We thought we could sing. We got a place in the chorus and for a while we done fine. Then the company laid off and it came summer and there was nuthin' we could do.

"We couldn't get work anywhere and we were hungry everlastin'. Poor Sadie kept a-moonin' around and thinkin' about Bob Parkins and prayin' he'd turn up for her like he said he would. She was plumb nutty about him and when we left he sed he'd come and git her if she didn't make good.

"After a while I couldn't stand it no longer and I went out to git some grub. I didn't give a darn how I got it. But Sadie wouldn't come. She said she couldn't break Bob's heart. He was bound to come. I came back in a coupla weeks. I'd made a penny. I thought I'd stake Sade to the fare back home. She was gone. She'd give up hopin' for Bob, and just made away with herself. Took the gas route in that very room where we used to stay."

Porter was pouring out the coffee and taking in every word.

"I guess Bob never showed up, did he?"

"Yes, he turned up one day. Said he'd been lookin' high and low for us. Been to every boarding house in the town searchin' for Sade. I hated to tell him. Gee, he never said a word for the longest time.

"Then he asked me all about Sade and if she'd carried on and why she hadn't let him know. I told him everything. All he said was 'Here, Sue, buy yerself some grub'.

"He gave me five dollars and me and Mame paid the rent and we been eatin' on it since. That was a week ago. I haven't seen Bob since. He was awful cut up about it."

Sue talked on in short, jerky sentences, but Porter was no longer paying the slightest attention to her. Suddenly he got up, went over to a small table and came back with a copy of "Cabbages and Kings."

"You might read this when you get time and tell me what you think of it."

The supper was finished. Porter seemed anxious to be rid of us all. The girls were quite pleased to leave. The little one looked regretfully at the bread and meat left on the table.

"You got plenty for breakfast!"

There was a paper on the chair. I shoved the food into it and tied it up. "Take it with you." Sue was embarrassed.

"Mame! For Gawd's sake, ain't you greedy!"
Mame laughed.

"Rainy day like to come any time for us."

Porter was preoccupied. He scarcely noticed that
they were gone. The idea had been tracked. It
possessed him. He already smelled the fragrance of
mignonette.

Sue had yielded her story to the magician. It went
through the delicate mill of his mind. It came out in
the wistful realism of "The Furnished Room."

CHAPTER XXIX.

Quest for material; Pilsner and the Halberdier; suggestion of a story; dining with editors; tales of train-robberies; a mood of despair.

If Porter caught the Voice of the City as no other has; if he reached the veins leading to its heart, it is because he was an inveterate prospector, forever hurling his pick into the asphalt. He struck it rich in the streets and the restaurants of Manhattan. Running through the hard-faced granite of its materialism, he came upon the deep shaft of romance and poetry.

Shot through the humdrum strata, the mellow gold of humor and pathos glinted before his eyes. New York was his Goldfield. But his lucky strike was muscled by Relentless Purpose, not Chance. No story-writer ever worked more persistently than O. Henry. He was the Insatiable Explorer.

The average man adopts a profession or a trade. In his leisure he is glad to turn his attention to other hobbies. With O. Henry, his work made up the sum total of his life. The two were inseparable.

He could no more help noticing and observing and mentally stocking up than a negative could avoid recording an image when the light strikes it. He had a mind that innately selected and recounted the story.

Sometimes he came upon the gold already separated, as in the story Sue told him. Sometimes there was but a sparkle. In fact, it was seldom that he took things as he found them.

His gravel went through many a wash before it came out O. Henry's unalloyed gold. What would have been but so much crushed rock for another, gleamed with nugget dust for him. So it was with "the Halberdier of the Little Rheinschloss."

"I'll introduce you to Pilsner," he said to me one night, when we started out on our rounds. "You'll like it better than your coffee strong enough to float your bandit bullets."

We went to a German restaurant on Broadway. We took a little table near the foot of the stairs. In one of his stories O. Henry says that "the proudest consummation of a New Yorker's ambition is to shake hands with a spaghetti chef or to receive a nod from a Broadway head waiter." That mark of deference was often his.

The Pilsner was good, but the thing of chief interest to me was a ridiculous figure standing at the landing of the stairs tricked out as an ancient Halberdier. I couldn't take my glance from him. He had the shiftiest eyes and the weakest hands. The contrast to his mighty coat of steel was laughable.

"Look at that weak-kneed saphead, Bill. Picture him as an ancient man-at-arms!" His fingers were yellow with nicotine to the knuckles.

Porter looked at him, sat back, finished his beer in silence. "It's a good story." That was all he said. We went home early and both of us were sober. Whenever this happened we used to sit in Bill's room and talk until one or two o'clock. This night it was different.

"Are you sleepy tonight, colonel?" he said. "I think I shall retire."

Whenever his mind was beset with an idea he lapsed into this extremely formal manner of speaking. It was bitterly irritating to me. I would leave in a kind of huff determined not to bother him again. But I knew that he was not conscious of his coldness. He was remote because his thought had built a barrier about him. He could think of nothing but the story in his mind.

I had an appointment with him for noon time. I decided not to keep it unless he remembered. At about 10 minutes after 12 he called me up.

"You're late. I'm waiting," he said.

When I got to his room the big table where he did his writing was littered with sheets of paper. All over the floor were scraps of paper covered with writing in long hand.

"When I get the returns on this I'll divvy up with you." Porter picked up a thick wad of sheets.

"Why?"

"It was you that gave me the thought."

"You mean the cigarette fiend in the armor?"

"Yes; I've just finished the yarn."

He read it to me. Just the merest glint had come to him from that steel-plated armor. The Halberdier himself would never have recognized the gem Porter's genius had polished for him. The story just as it stands today was written by Porter some time between midnight and noon.

And yet he looked as fresh and rested as though he had slept ten hours.

"Do you always grab off an inspiration like that and dash it off without any trouble?"

Porter opened a drawer in the desk. "Look at those." He pointed to a crammed-down heap of papers covered with his long freehand.

"Sometimes I can't make the story go and I lay it away for a happier moment. There is a lot of unfinished business in there that will have to be transacted some day. I don't dash off stories. I'm always thinking about them, and I seldom start to write until the thing is finished in my mind. It doesn't take long to set it down."

I have watched him sit with pencil poised sometimes for hours, waiting for the story to tell itself to his brain.

O. Henry was a careful artist. He was a slave to the dictionary. He would pore over it, taking an infinite relish in the discovery of a new twist to a word.

One day he was sitting at the table with his back to me. He had been writing with incredible rapidity, as though the words just ran themselves automatically from his pen. Suddenly he stopped. For half an hour he sat silent, and then he turned around, rather surprised to find me still there.

"Thirsty, colonel? Let's get a drink."

"Bill," my curiosity was up, "does your mind feel a blank when you sit there like that?" The question seemed to amuse him.

"No. But I have to reason out the meaning of words."

There was no ostentation in Porter, either in his writing or in his observations. I never saw him making notes in public, except once in a while he would jot a word down on the corner of a napkin.

He didn't want other people to know what he was thinking about. He didn't need to take notes, for he was not a procrastinator. He transmuted his thoughts into stories while the warm beat throbbed in them.

Careless and irresponsible as he seemed—almost aimless at times—I think there was in Bill Porter a purposiveness that was grim and so determined that he would allow no external influence to interfere with his plan of life.

I have sometimes felt that this passionate will to be himself at all times made him so aloof and reclusive. He sought companionship freely with strangers, for he could dispense with their company at will. He wanted to live untrammeled. And he did. He was incorrigibly stubborn-minded. Of all the men I have ever known, Bill Porter ran truest to the natural grain.

As soon as New York became aware of O. Henry's lucky strike, it was ready with its meed of homage. An eager, rushing multitude sought him out. Doors were flung wide. The man who had but a few years before been separated from his fellows could now stand among the proudest, commanding, as he would, their smiles and their tears. He preferred solitude. Not because he disdained company—not that he feared exposure, but because he despised deceit and hypocrisy. And these, he felt, were the inevitable attendants of men and women in their social intercourse.

"Al, I despise these literati." Many a time he voiced the sentiment. "They remind me of big balloons. If one were to puncture their pose, there would be an astonished gasp as when one sticks a pin in the stretched rubber. And then they would be no more—not even a wrinkled trace of them!"

They could sue him with invitations. He had no time to waste. He was not vain, and never did he consciously try to impress any one. He was not of that righteous type that takes itself and its beliefs with ponderous seriousness, insisting that the world hear them out and then applaud.

Bill Porter was too busy watching others to take much heed about his own reflection. Because he was eminently self-sufficient, he would not allow circumstances to set his friendships for him.

But with the few who were the elect to him; who knew him and understood him he was the droll and beloved vagabond. Reticence would drop from him. He was in his element—the troubadour of old, the sparkle of his gracious wit bubbling through every breath of the heavier discourse.

"I have a treat for you, colonel. Tonight you shall meet the Chosen Few."

He would tell me no more, seeming to take a boyish delight in my irritable suspense. The Chosen Few happened to be Richard Duffy, Gilman Hall and Bannister Merwin. We had dinner together at the Hoffman House.

It was a treat—for that night I saw O. Henry as he might have been if the buoyant happiness that seemed to be his native disposition had not been deepened and saddened by the distressing humiliation of his prison years.

Porter handed me the ménu. He was a bit finicky about his eating. "Gentlemen," he said to the distinguished editors, "the colonel will pick out a surprise for us." I think Porter considered me somewhat brazen because I was not awed by this presence of the élite.

"I could order bacon broiled on the hickory coals, terrapin, sour-dough biscuit and coffee strong enough to float the bullets—how would you like it, Bill?"

"Don't endanger my future in my chosen profession by making me hit the tracks for the West."

Duffy and Hall looked at Porter as though a sudden vision of his portly figure galloped before them on horseback and swinging a lariat. Porter caught the question in their eyes. He was in a tantalizing mood.

"You wouldn't mind edifying the company with a discourse on the ethics of train-robbing, would you, colonel?" The three guests sat up, tense with interest. It was just the setting I loved. It gave me a big bump of joy to throw a shock into those blasé New Yorkers.

Yarn after yarn I reeled off for their absorption. I told them all the funny incidents connected with the stickup of the trains in the Indian Territory.

I made them see the outlaw, not as a ruthless brute, but as a human being possessed of a somewhat different bias or viewpoint from their own. Porter sat back, expansive and sedate, with his large gray eye lighted with amusement.

"Colonel, I stood in your shadow tonight," he said to me as we were parting at the Caledonia.

"What do you mean, Bill?"

"My friends to whom I introduced you ignored me. I was rather some pumpkins with Hall and Duffy until you came, and tonight I was forgotten by them. Would you mind the next time we are together telling them I held the horses for you?"

"Honest, Bill, do you mean it?"

"Yes, I think it would add to my prestige."

A few days later we were at Mouquin's. I was stringing out a lurid outlaw story. I stopped in the middle and turned to Porter, as though my memory had slipped and I had overlooked an important detail. "Bill, you remember," I said, "that was the night you held the horses." Duffy dropped his fork, sending out a roar of laughter. He reached over and grabbed Porter's hand. "By Jove, I always suspected you, Bill Porter."

"I want to thank you, colonel, for those kind words. You have done me a great service. I sold two stories this morning on the strength of my presumed association with you," Porter said a day later. "Those fellows think now that I really belonged to your gang. I have become a personage."

Not for worlds, though, would Porter have openly acknowledged to these men that he had been a prisoner in the Ohio penitentiary. Bob Davis, I am certain, knew it. He practically admitted it to me. Duffy and Hall felt the mystery surrounding the man.

"Colonel, every time I step into a public café I have the horrible fear that some ex-con will come up and say to me 'Hello, Bill; when did you get out of the O. P.'?"

No one ever did this. It would have been an insufferable shock to Porter's pride, especially when his success was new to him. After all the jovial warmth of that dinner at Mouquin's, after all the banter and gayety, the weight of oppressive sadness came down upon him.

The memory of the past; the troubled fear of the future—the two together seemed ever to press like gigantic forces against the bonny happiness of the present for Bill Porter.

I was recklessly gay. I had taken plenty of the "wine that boils when it is cold." In the exuberance I asked all the gentlemen present to be my escort across the river. Porter kicked me under the table, turning on me a straight, meaningful look.

"Colonel, I am the only one that has nothing to do except yourself. These gentlemen are editors. I shall be glad to act as your escort and keep you from walking off the boat. The sea never gives up its dead."

"I didn't want those men to be with us in our last moments," he said when we were crossing the Hudson.

"Good God, Bill, you aren't going to jump over and pull me with you?"

"No. But I think I would rather enjoy it."

He had not been shamming gayety at the dinner. When a full tide, it had swept over him. But there was always an undertow of shadows and whenever he was alone it carried him out—often to a bitter depth of gloomy depression.

CHAPTER XXX.

A human prism he was—refracting the light in seven different colors. But different in this—he was not predictable. Reds and blues and yellows were in his moods, but sometimes the gold would predominate and sometimes the indigo. Bill Porter's was a baffling spectrum of gay and somber hues.

These moods of his were inscrutable to me. At times he was so aloof I could scarcely get a word from him. I would go away seething with anger. And in an hour he would come over with the gentlest and subtlest persuasion to wheedle me into friendliness.

"Bill, you've got a feminine streak in you; you're so damned unreliable." I meant it for a stinging rebuke.

Porter looked at me, putting on a foolish simper. "It makes me quite interesting and enigmatic, doesn't it, colonel?"

And then he became instantly serious. "Sometimes things look so black to me, Al. I don't see much use in anything. I can't bet on myself. Sometimes I want to have nothing to do with any one and sometimes I envy the defiance that seems to win you so many friends."

Porter could have walked down Broadway and won

the smiling salute of every celebrity for a mile had he
so wished. And yet he made that comment one day
because a half-dozen bartenders had called me by
name.

He had been very busy getting out some stories. I
had not seen him for four days. I improved the time
by striking up acquaintance with the élite of the bar-
rooms. One evening I was talking to the tender in a
saloon across from the Flatiron Building. Both my
listener and I were excitedly going through the peril-
ous joys of a holdup. I heard a hesitating cough.
Porter was at my elbow.

"Did you find an old friend in the bartender?" he
asked when we got outside.

"No, I just met him yesterday."

"Well, I stood there 10 minutes with a Sahara
thirst on me before he turned to quench it. You're
evidently more riches to him than my dime.

"I've been looking for you, colonel. I went into
five different saloons. I asked if a diminutive giant
with a demure face and red hair had been prowling
about the premises. 'Who, Mr. Jennings from Oklahoma?' they up and says, and then they try to point
out your footprints to me on the asphalt. How do
you do it?

"You ought to come here and run for Mayor. You'd
be elected sure. And then you could appoint me your
secretary. We'd be in clover."

Many hours later we wheeled around again near
the Flatiron Building. My hat was carried away in
the tornado and then hurled down the street.

I started to run after it. Porter's firm, strong hand

was on my arm. "Don't, colonel. Some one will bring it to you. The north wind is considerate. It pays indemnities on the damage wrought. It will send a porter to return your headpiece to you."

"Like hell it will."

A likely chance it seemed at two o'clock in the morning. I shook off his arm, determined to recover my property, when dashing up from nowhere came an old man. "Pardon me, sir, is this yours?"

For the second time in my life I heard Bill Porter send up that bubbling, sonorous laugh of his.

For a moment I felt like a person bewitched. "Where in thunder did that old gnome come from, anyway?"

"You oughtn't to be so particular about the creature's origin. You've got your hat, haven't you?"

It was a night of gayety. "We'll continue this in our next, colonel. Come over at noon." It was Porter's good night.

I was ready for the jaunt promptly at 12. "Mr. Porter is in his rooms—go right up," the clerk said. I reached the door. I could hear Bill stropping his razor. I knocked. He did not answer.

Mindful of the joyous buoyancy of the night before I gave a vicious kick at the door. He did not come.

In a gale of resentment and hurt pride, I rushed to my room a block away.

"He's sick and tired of me sliding in there night and day," I thought. "He wants to be rid of me." I grabbed up my suitcase and started dumping my clothes into it. I planned to leave New York that afternoon. I was just jamming in the last few collars when the door opened and Bill's ruddy, understanding face looked down at me.

"Forgive me, colonel, that I have not a sixth sense. I could not distinguish your knock from any one else's." Porter slipped his hand into his pocket. "Take this, Al, and let yourself in any hour of the day or night. You'll never find Bill Porter's door or his time locked against the salt of the earth."

More eloquent than the gift of a dollar from a Shylock was this tribute from the reserved Bill Porter.

I was always under the impression that Porter's spirit, unshadowed by the walls of the Ohio penitentiary, would have been a buoyant, fantastic incarnation. He had a robust philosophy that withstood without the tarnish of cynicism the horrors of prison life.

Without these searing memories I think the debonair grace of youth that was uppermost in his heart would have been the dominant force triumphant over the ordinary melancholy of life.

"I have accepted an invitation for you, colonel." He was in one of his gently sparkling moods. "Get into your armor asinorum, for we fare forth to make contest with tinsel and gauze. In other words we mingle with the proletariat. We go to see Margaret Anglin and Henry Miller in that superb and realistic Western libel, 'The great Divide'."

After the play the great actress, Porter and I and one or two others were to have supper at the Breslin Hotel. I think Porter took me there that he might sit back and enjoy my unabashed criticisms to the lady's face.

"I feel greatly disappointed in you, Mr. Porter,"

Margaret Anglin said to Bill as we took our places at the table.

"In what have I failed?"

"You promised to bring your Western friend—that terrible outlaw Mr. Jennings—to criticise the play."

"Well, I have introduced him." He waved his hand down toward me.

Miss Anglin looked me over with the trace of a smile in her eye.

"Pardon me," she said, "but I can hardly associate you with the lovely things they say of you. Did you like the play?"

I told her I didn't. It was unreal. No man of the West would shake dice for a lady in distress. The situation was unheard of and could only occur in the imagination of a fat-headed Easterner who had never set his feet beyond the Hudson.

Miss Anglin laughed merrily. "New York is wild over it. New York doesn't know any better."

Porter sat back, an expansive smile spreading a light in his gray eyes. "I am inclined to agree with our friend," he offered. "The West is unacquainted with Manhattan chivalry." Afterward he kept prodding every one present with his genial quips.

I never saw him in a happier mood. The very next morning he was in the depths of despondency. I went over early in the afternoon. He was sitting at his desk rigid and silent. I started to tiptoe out. I thought he was concentrated in his writing.

"Come in, Al." He had a picture in his hand. "That's Margaret, colonel. I want you to have the picture. If anything should happen to me, I think I'd feel happy if you would look after her."

He seemed crushed and hopeless. He went over to the window and looked out.

"You know I kind of like this old dismal city of dying souls."

"What the hell has that got to do with your kicking off?"

"Nothing, but the jig is up. Colonel, have you the price? Let's have a little refreshment. They'll be up with a check some time, I hope."

I did not know the cause of his sudden overpowering dejection, but no drink could lighten it. The light-hearted, winsome joyousness of the night before had vanished. The bright hues in the spectrum were muddled into the drab.

One night—a cold, raw, angry night—Bill and I were strolling along somewhere in the East Side. "Remember the kid they electrocuted at the O. P.?" he said to me. "I will show you life tonight that is more tragic than death."

Faces that were no longer human—that seemed scarred and blemished as though the skin were a kind of web-like scale—dodged from alleyways and basements.

"They are the other side of the Enchanted Profile. You don't see it on our God. He keeps it hidden."

To Bill, long before he had written the story of that name, the Enchanted Profile was the face on the dollar.

We were turning a dingy corner. The sorriest, forlornest slice of tatterdemalion came shambling along. He was sober. Hunger—if you've ever felt it, you recognize in the other fellow's eyes—stared out from his emaciated face. "Hello, pard." Bill stepped to his side and slipped a bill into his hand. We went on. A moment later the hobo shuffled up. "'Scuse me, mister. You made a mistake. You gave me $20."

"Who told you I made a mistake?" Porter pushed him. "Be off."

And the next day he asked me to walk four blocks out of our way to get a drink.

"We need the exercise. We're getting obese." I noticed that the bartender greeted Bill with a familiar smile. At the counter a big fat man jostled me, nearly knocking the glass from my hand.

It made me furious. I swung my fist. Porter caught my arm. "They don't mean anything, these New York hogs."

It happened again and again. The fourth time Porter asked me to go there I became curious.

"What do you like about that rough joint, Bill?"

"I'm broke, colonel, and the bartender knows me. My credit there is unlimited."

Broke—yet he had $20 to throw away to a bum! Porter had no conception of money values. He seemed to act according to some super standard of his own.

He beggared himself financially with his spend-thrift ways, but his whimsical investments brought him in a rich store of experience and satisfaction. The wealth of his self-expression was worth more to him than economic affluence.

Yet he was not one who bore amiably an empty wallet. He liked to spend. He wished always to be the host. Often he would say to me, "I shall have the pleasure of ordering this at your expense." When the meal was finished I would look for the check, picking up the napkins and fussing about.

"Cease your ostentation," he would say. "That is paid and forgotten. Don't make such a vulgar display of wealth."

He liked to spend—but he liked better to give away. In the book he had given to Sue he had slipped a $10 bill. She came back a few days later after the banquet at the Caledonia. I was waiting for Porter.

"I've come to bring this back. Your friend, Mr. Bill, forgot to look before he gave it to me." Just then Porter came in.

"Good morning, Miss Sue." I had forgotten her name and was calling her Sophie and Sarah and honey. Porter doffed the cap he was wearing.

"Will you come in?"

"I just come to hand this back." Porter looked at the note in her hand as though he considered himself the victim of a practical joker.

"What is the meaning of this?"

"It was in the book you give me."

"It does not belong to me, Sue. You must have put it there and forgotten."

The girl smiled, but into her intelligent black eyes came a look of gratitude and understanding.

"Forgotten, Mr. Bill? If you'd only handled as few ten spots as I have you couldn't no wise misplace one without knowin' it."

"It's yours, Sue, for I know it isn't mine. But, say, Sue, some day I might be hard up and I'll come around and get you to stake me to a meal. And if you're out of luck, ring this bell."

"There ain't many like you gents." The girl's face was flushed with gladness. "Mame and me, we think you're princes."

Half way down the hall she turned. "I know it's yours, Bill. Thanks."

CHAPTER XXXI.

After two years; a wedding invitation; another visit to New York; delayed hospitality; in O. Henry's home; blackmail.

A hastily scrawled note accompanied a formal invitation. It was a bid to the wedding of William Sydney Porter and Miss Sallie Coleman, of Asheville, N. C.

Bill Porter, the prowler, the midnight investigator, the devil-may-care Bohemian was going to squeeze himself into the tight-cut habit of the benedict. When I read that note I felt as though I had been asked to a funeral.

It was more than two years since I had seen Bill. Son of impulse and whim that he was, who could figure this new venture of his?

"Pack up your togs, colonel, and come to the show. It won't be complete without you."

For months I had been planning another trip to New York. I wanted to get my book into print. Porter kept encouraging me. That was one glorious trait in him. If he saw a spark of talent in another he would fan it with praise and encouragement.

A thousand suggestions he had given me. Short stories that I had written, he had taken personally to editors and tried to make a sale for me. Another trip to New York, another joyous pilgrimage into the Mystic Maze with the Magician of Bagdad at my side—if I had any talent it would surely be kindled into flame.

The little note I held in my hand was like a heavy wet blanket on the fire of that hope. My wife and I went to the finest store in Oklahoma and bought some kind of a cut-glass water set. I sent the requisite "Congratulations and Best Wishes." There ends the greatness of Bill Porter, I thought. I was mistaken.

Toward the middle of December Porter returned a rejected manuscript to me.

"Don't give up, colonel. I'm sure you could make good at short stories. Come to New York. Don't build any high hopes on your book. Just consider you're on a little pleasure trip and taking it along as a side line. Mighty few manuscripts ever get to be books and mighty few books pay. Let me know in advance a day or two when you will arrive. Louisa is in Grand Rapids. Maybe he will run over for a day or two."

Less than a week later I was in New York. As soon as I arrived I called him up. I may have imagined it, but he did not seem like the old Bill to me. He was busy on a story.

"I'll call you up and let you buy the drinks as soon as the manuscript is finished."

Porter was an earnest worker. Pleasure never lured him from his desk, perhaps because he found such a joy in writing.

A week passed. I did not hear from him.

"He doesn't want me around his proud Southern wife," I thought. "Bill has put the convict number behind him. I've flaunted mine. This marriage of his may help him to forget. He probably doesn't want any red-headed reminder bobbing around."

As usual I had to take back the hasty judgment.

Richard Duffy came over for me one evening.

"Bill wants to see you. We're all going to dinner together."

We got to the Caledonia, where he still kept his study. Porter was at his desk, dashing in a last few periods. He looked tired, as though he had been under a long strain.

"I've been working like the devil, Bill. I've been feeling very tired. Join me in a drink. Will that make amends?"

"I don't know that any amends are necessary." I felt irritated and showed it. On the way to Mouquin's we scarcely spoke. I felt a kind of estrangement. But after the dinner the old, sunny familiarity melted the coldness.

"I'd like you to meet my wife, colonel."

Somehow I felt the words were not the truth. I all but said I didn't want to see her. I felt that she would not welcome an ex-convict.

The graciousness of Southern hospitality dispelled my fears. We reached Porter's apartments about 10:30, an hour and a half late. Mrs. Porter greeted us with great cordiality. She had been the first love of Porter in his boyhood days.

To admit the least, I was slightly "teed." Perhaps she did not observe it. Certainly there was no hint of disapproval in her manner.

She served us refreshments and chatted with a pleasant ease. I was relieved, but not convinced.

Toward midnight Duffy and I started to leave. Bill took up his hat.

"Why, you're not going, too, are you, Mr. Porter?" the lady said.

He stopped for a moment to explain. Duffy and I walked up the street.

"What the hell did Bill want with a wife? It puts an end to his liberty—his wanderings," I whispered loudly to Duffy, just as Porter tapped me on the shoulder. He smiled expansively, irrepressibly, as a boy might have.

"You're not pleased with my choice?"

"I'm not to be pleased!" I fired back.

I intended walking on with Duffy. Porter interfered.

"Come this way with me. We may not see much more of each other."

We went down to the Hudson and sat on the docks. The lights of all New Jersey, like a million stars, like a hundred Milky Ways, sparkled in the water. The big steamers, black, powerful, were moored in the slips. Tugboats and ferries skimmed—mystic, enchanted barks—up and down the river.

We talked carelessly. Porter started several times to speak seriously and broke off. Another mood seized him and he looked at me indulgently and smiled.

"You're dissatisfied with my matrimonial venture?"

"It's the silliest thing you ever did."

"She is a most estimable young lady." Porter seemed to be enjoying my resentment.

"That may be, but what did you want with her?"

"I loved her."

"Oh, my God! That covers a multitude of sins."

Porter was a born troubadour. He had a happy-go-lucky heart, for all that it was crowded down with sadness. I felt that he had made a fatal mistake to take upon himself obligations that his nature made him unfitted to meet.

"Colonel, I wanted your opinion. I've wondered if I acted honorably."

Porter was the soul of chivalry. For all that he saw in Hell's Kitchen, his reverence for woman remained. "I've married a highbred woman and brought all my troubles upon her. Was it right?"

Strange blend of impulsiveness and honor, the instinctive nobility in Porter urged him always to measure up to his big responsibilities.

My fears were ill founded. Bill's marriage did not interfere with his greatness. He was never one of the recklessly debonair who shake off with an easy conscience the obligations they have incurred. Porter served two masters—Bohemianism, Convention. He served both well.

Only the Midas touch or the purse of Fortunatus could answer such demands. It does not need the suggestion of blackmail to account for Porter's intermittent penury. But I know that in one instance he was a victim.

It was the night after his sudden despondency. For three hours I sat in his room waiting for him to keep an appointment. He came in whitefaced and haggard. The jaunty neatness that was always his was gone. He looked limp and careless to me. He went over to his desk and sat down. After a long silence he faced

me. "I was serious, colonel, last night. If I should
drop off, will you look after Margaret—be a sort of
foster-father, as it were?"

"What's up, Bill? You're as husky as a stevedore."

"Colonel, you were right. I should have faced it."
And, without prelude, he launched into the most unusual confidence. Twice Porter deliberately spoke of
his own affairs.

"I can't stand it much longer. She comes after me
regularly, and she's the wife of a big broker here at
that. Tonight I told her to go hang. She'll get no
more from me."

"Will she tell?"

"Let her."

Not a former convict at the penitentiary—none of
these, so far as I know, ever bothered him—but a
woman of high social class, a woman who had lived
in Austin and flirted with Bill Porter in his troubadour
days.

"We used to sing under her window, once in a
while. She came to me months ago. She knew my
whole history. She came as a friend.

"She was in terrible straits, she said. Her Southern
pride wouldn't let her ask any of her circle. She
wanted a thousand. I had $150 Gilman Hall had sent
me. I let her have it. She has been to see me regularly
ever since. I've emptied my pockets on that table for
her. Now I'm through. I could have killed her."

I knew the violence of anger that had once before
swept Bill Porter when he leaped at the Spanish don.
He sat back now, spent and nerveless. But I was
afraid to leave him alone. I stayed there all night.

"She'll never trouble you, Bill. You should have called her bluff the first time. You've nothing to lose."

"I have much to lose, colonel. I don't look at things as you do."

The incident was closed. The woman did not bother him again, but Porter's ups and downs continued their unhappy succession.

Not blackmail, but fantastic liberality kept his pocket empty. To many a down-and-outer he must have seemed a veritable "scattergold."

I remember one quaint, elfin-faced girl. Porter supported both her and her mother.

"They were very kind to me when I had no friends in Pittsburgh," he said to me one evening, when he brought the girl to dinner with us at Mouquin's. "They came to New York and were stranded. I am but meeting an obligation."

I could see nothing to this skimpy brown remnant of a girl. She looked like a wistful little gypsy. But Porter loved her, and she worshiped him with the fidelity of a dog. She used to send him odd, outlandish presents that were an abomination to his cultured taste. But he would pretend to like them.

She was bright and happy, but she had little to say. Many a time the three of us had dinner together in New York on my first visit. There was a certain fairy-like charm to her—she was so unobtrusive. We scarcely noticed her presence. She was content to listen in smiling quiet to Porter's talk.

When he spoke to her it was with the gentle deference due a queen.

One night he put a red and green handkerchief in

his coat pocket. I looked at him amazed. Rich, harmonious colors were his preference. He smiled.

"She sent it up to me. I don't wish to wound her."

Prince, then pauper, Prodigal one day—broke the next. Whim was his bookkeeper. It piled a big deficit on the prosy, matter-of-fact side of the ledger, but it splashed the inner, realer pages with a bounteous, unaccountable credit. With a higher kind of reckoning it gave us Bill Porter—reckless of the superficial values; unerring in his devotion to the better standard as he saw it.

CHAPTER XXXII.

New Year's eve; the last talk; "a missionary after all."

As one who stood in the world's highway while the rushing multitude in the ever shifting pageant of Life went by, each scene flashing upon the vivid negative of his mind a new record, each picture different, unexpected, developing new lights and shades—like that in his relation to Life was Bill Porter.

For him there could be no monotony, no "world overrun by conclusions, no life moving by rote." Ever new, ever incalculable, ever absorbing—the moving drama gripped his mind with its humor and its tragedy; it held his heart with its joy and its sadness. Desolate it was at times and piercing in its pathos—uninteresting or dull, never. Porter lived in a quivering, tense excitement, for he was one who watched and in a little understood the vast hubbub of striving, half-blind humanity.

He had about him an air of suspense, of throbbing expectancy, as though he had just concluded an adventure or were just about to set forth on one. Whenever I saw him I had an instinctive question on my lips—"What's up, Bill?"

His attitude piqued curiosity. I felt it the day he came down from the veranda of the American consulate and began, in that low-pitched voice, the droll and solemn dissertation on the Mexican liquor situation.

It was with him through the dreary unhappiness of the prison years and in the big struggle to come back in New York. In every turn of that devious route, even through the noisome tunnel, he strode with brave and questing tread. Life never bored him. From the first moment I met him until the last he never lost interest.

"You shall have a strange and bewildering experience tonight, my brave bandit, and I shall have the joy of watching you."

It was the last day of 1907. For hours I had sat in Porter's room in the Caledonia, waiting for him to finish his work. He was writing with lightning speed. Sometimes he would finish a page and immediately wrinkle it into a ball and throw it on the floor. Then he would write on, page after page, with hardly a pause, or he would sit silent and concentrated for half an hour at a stretch. I was weary of waiting.

"But there is still something new in the world, Al," he promised. "You'll get a shock that all the bumptious thrills of train-robbing never afforded."

It was almost midnight when we started forth.

He led me through alleys and by-streets I had never seen. We came into dark, narrow lanes, where old five- and six-story residences, dilapidated and neglected, sent forth an ancient musty odor. We went on and on until it seemed that we had reached the bottom of a black, unfathomable hole in the very center of the city.

"Listen," he whispered. And in a moment a wild,

whistling tumult, that was as if the horns and trumpets and all the mighty bells of heaven and earth let loose a shouting thunder, came down into that hole and caught it in a shrieking boom. I reached out my hand and touched Porter's arm. "My God, Bill, what is it?"

"Something new under the moon, colonel, whenever you can't find it under the sun. That, friend, is but New York's greeting to the New Year."

That hole—and no one but the Prowling Magician in his everlasting search for the otherwise could have found it—was somewhere near the Hudson.

"Do you feel that a little conversation in my soothing pianissimo would revive you, colonel?"

We went down to the docks and sat there for an hour before we spoke a word. It was the last long communion I was ever to have with the gifted friend, whose memory has been and is an inspiration.

Porter seemed suddenly to be wrapped in gloom. I was leaving in a day or two. Moved by some unaccountable impulse—perhaps by the melancholy in his manner, I suggested that he accompany me."

"I'd like to go West and over the beaten paths with you. When I can make better provision for those dependent on me, I may."

"Oh, just cut loose and come. I'll take you out among all the old timers. You can get material enough to run you ten years on Western stories."

I was rambling on vividly. Porter's warm, strong hand clasped mine.

"Colonel," he interrupted, "I have a strange idea that this will be our last meeting." With a quick change of mood, he smiled sheepishly. "Besides, I have not yet converted New York."

Converted—I laughed at that word from Bill Porter. I remembered his flashing resentment when I suggested the rôle to him before he left the penitentiary.

"So you did become a missionary after all! What effect do you think "The Four Million" will have on the readers in this maelstrom? Will it reach out and correct evils?"

"That is too much to ask. The blind will not perceive its message."

"Blind—who do you mean by that?"

"Not the idle poor, colonel, but the idle rich. They will yet live to have the bandage torn by gaunt, angry hands from their lazy, unseeing eyes."

"Where did you get that hunch, Bill?"

"In our former residence, colonel."

Mellowed and broadened, he was this man who came back from the blighting tunnel to the welcoming highways. A different Bill, this friend of the shopgirl and down-and-outer, from the proud recluse who stopped his ears to Sallie's needs and shuddered with abhorrence at the mere mention of the Prison Demon.

"I haven't changed colonel; but I see more. Life seems to me like a rich, vast diamond that is forever flashing new facets before us. I never tire of watching it. When my own future seemed so black—that interest kept me going."

For all his whims and his fine, high pride, for all the sadness that was often his, this interest kept him forever on tiptoe. He was never a laggard in the fine art of living.

Bill Porter had a sort of corner on the romance of life—a monopoly that was his by the divine right of understanding. It was a light that rifled even the sordid murk of the basement café and turned upon the hidden worth in the character of the starved and wretched dancing girls.

If life brought an ever new thrill to him he returned to it a gentle radiance that made glad the heart of many a Sue, many a Soapy.

There was in him a sunny toleration—an eager youthfulness. He was the great adventurer with his hand on life's pulse-beat.

To have stood at his side and looked through his eyes has softened with mellow humor the stark and cruel things—has touched with disturbing beauty the finer elements of existence.

THE END.